Judy Garton-Sprenger and Philip Prowse
with Helena Gomm

Workbook 1

Welcome!

1 Reading

Read the dialogue. Then complete the sentences.

DAVID   Hi, everyone. It's nice to meet you. I'm David Ward. This is Emily and this is Adam.
EMILY   Hello.
ADAM   Hello. Welcome to Brighton.
PIERRE Hi, I'm Pierre.
ADAM   Are you from Spain?
PIERRE No, I'm not. I'm from Switzerland.
TERESA Hi, I'm Teresa. I'm from Spain.
ADAM   It's nice to meet you.
JAKE   Hi, I'm Jake.
PIERRE Are you from England?
JAKE   No, I'm not. I'm from the USA.
KATYA   And I'm from Russia. I'm Katya.

1 Pierre _is_ from Switzerland.
2 David, Emily and Adam _____ from England.
3 Jake isn't from _____. He's from _____.
4 _____ Pierre from Spain? No, he isn't.
5 Who is _____ Russia? Katya.

2 Present simple of be

Write sentences about these famous people.

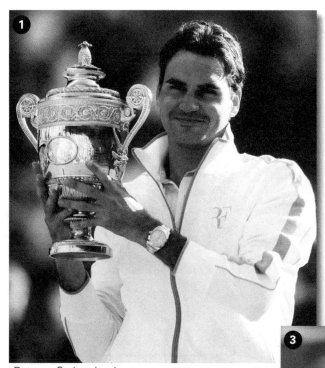

Roger – Switzerland

This is Roger and he's from Switzerland.

Alicia – the USA

Rafael – Spain

Ksenia – Russia

Daniel – England

Welcome!

3 Present simple of be
Complete. Then write sentences.

I'm from Spain.

.... from Switzerland.

.... from England.

3 ....

.... from Russia.

.... from the USA.

1 *She's from Spain.*

2 ....

3 ....

4 ....

5 ....

4 Present simple of be
Write questions and then answer them.

1 Emily and Adam/American
   Are Emily and Adam American?
   No, they aren't. They're English.

2 Katya/English
   ....
   ....

3 Pierre/Russian
   ....
   ....

4 Teresa/Swiss
   ....
   ....

5 Jake/Spanish
   ....
   ....

6 David/American
   ....
   ....

7 you/English
   ....
   No, I'm not. I'm ....

5 Present simple of be
Rewrite the sentences using the full form of be.

1 What's your name? *What is your name?*
2 He's a teacher. ....
3 We're students. ....
4 I'm not American. ....
5 Who's she? ....
6 They're English. ....
7 She isn't a teacher. ....
8 You're at school. ....
9 It's nice to meet you. ....
10 We aren't in Brighton. ....

6 Possessive adjectives

Complete with *my*, *your*, *his* and *her*.

EMILY What's (**1**) ___your___ name?

TERESA (**2**) _____ name is Teresa.

EMILY What's the name of the girl from Russia?

TERESA (**3**) _____ name is Katya.

EMILY And what's the name of the Swiss boy?

TERESA (**4**) _____ name is Pierre.

7 Vocabulary

Find the words for numbers 1–10 in the word square.

T	H	R	E	E	Q
E	S	O	S	I	F
N	I	N	E	G	O
M	X	E	V	H	U
F	I	V	E	T	R
T	W	O	N	P	D

8 Vocabulary

Write the answers in words.

1 eleven + one = ___twelve___
2 twelve + seven = _____
3 nineteen – six = _____
4 ten + five = _____
5 twenty – four = _____
6 eight + six = _____
7 sixteen – five = _____
8 seven + thirteen = _____
9 twenty – two = _____
10 three + fourteen = _____

9 Vocabulary

Write the numbers.

zero ___0___   two _____
five _____   eight _____
twelve _____   fourteen _____
sixteen _____ twenty _____

Write the words.

1 ___one___   4 _____
7 _____ 9 _____
11 _____ 13 _____
15 _____ 18 _____

10 Vocabulary

Match the beginnings of the words with the endings. Then write the words.

1 add — ent   ___address___
2 num   come   _____
3 stud   her   _____
4 teac   end   _____
5 sch   ber   _____
6 wel   ress   _____
7 fri   ool   _____

11 Pronunciation

Find the rhyming words in the box.

I	he	they	street	~~who~~	your

1 two   ___who___
2 meet   _____
3 four   _____
4 three _____
5 my   _____
6 day   _____

> **Extension** Write three sentences about famous people in your notebook. Give their names and say where they are from.

1 NICE TO MEET YOU

1 That's a great bag!

1 Reading

Read the dialogue. Then complete the sentences.

JAKE	Hi, I'm Jake Turner.
KATYA	Nice to meet you, Jake. I'm Katya Petrova.
JAKE	Sorry, what's your surname?
KATYA	Petrova – it's a Russian name.
JAKE	How do you spell it?
KATYA	P-E-T-R-O-V-A.
JAKE	Oh, I see. Is that your bag?
KATYA	No, it isn't. There's Teresa. Is it her bag?
JAKE	Yes, I think it is.

Jake

1 His surname is _____.
2 He asks Katya how to _____ her surname.

Katya

3 _____ surname is Petrova.
4 It _____ her bag.

2 this/that

Look at the pictures and write questions with *this* or *that*.

1 *Is this your passport?*   2 *Is that your umbrella?*

3 _____   4 _____

5 _____   6 _____

7 _____   8 _____

9 _____   10 _____

3 Indefinite article *a/an*

Complete with *a* or *an*.

1 *an* ID card
2 _____ bottle
3 _____ rucksack
4 _____ alarm clock
5 _____ pen
6 _____ umbrella
7 _____ English girl
8 _____ MP3 player
9 _____ photo
10 _____ American boy

UNIT 1

4 Vocabulary

Look at the pictures and complete the sentences.

1 _It's called a_ digital _camera_ .
2 _____ MP3 _____ .
3 _____ alarm _____ .
4 _____ packet of _____ .
5 _____ mobile _____ .

5 Vocabulary

Find eight things in the word chain.

PHOTOPENCOMBOOKEYWALLETICKETPHONE

6 Vocabulary

What is it in English? Write sentences.

1 _It's a chair_ .

2 _____

3 _____

4 _____

5 _____

6 _____

7 Punctuation

Rewrite these questions and statements correctly.

1 whatsyourname
   What's your name?
2 isthatenglish
3 whatsthatcalled
4 itsmyMP3player
5 nowitsyourturn
6 thatsyourkey
7 wheresshefrom
8 whatsinit
9 wheresyourpassport
10 howdoyouspellit

8 Pronunciation

Which letters sound similar? Find the odd letter.

1 J (Z) K A
2 G P Y T
3 B D V I
4 Q H U W
5 N S X R
6 M L K F
7 O C E G

Extension In your notebook, write three sentences about what's in your bag.

1 NICE TO MEET YOU

2 How old is it?

1 Reading

Read the dialogue. Then read the sentences and write *T* (true) or *F* (false).

TERESA That's a great photo, Katya. Where is it?
KATYA   It's St Basil's Cathedral. It's in the centre of Moscow, in Red Square.
TERESA Wow, it's beautiful! How old is it?
KATYA   It's 450 years old. It's my favourite building.

1 The photo is of the Royal Pavilion. [F]
2 St Basil's Cathedral is in Brighton. □
3 St Basil's Cathedral is a beautiful building. □
4 St Basil's Cathedral is 450 years old. □
5 Teresa says St Basil's Cathedral is her favourite building. □

2 Reading

Look at the dialogue on page 14 of the Student's Book. Write questions for these answers.

1 *Where's the Royal Pavilion?*
  It's in Brighton, near the beach.
2 _____
  It's about 200 years old.
3 _____
  The London to Brighton Bike Ride is today.
4 _____
  It's at half past twelve.
5 _____
  It's twenty-five past twelve.
6 _____
  It's at quarter to seven tonight.

3 these/those and plural nouns

Rewrite these sentences in the plural.

1 That's your key. *Those are your keys.*
2 This is my friend. _____
3 This is your map. _____
4 That's your chair. _____
5 Is that his book? _____
6 This is her cat. _____
7 Is that your pen? _____
8 This is my wallet. _____

4 this/that and singular nouns

Rewrite these sentences in the singular.

1 Those are the tickets.
  That is the ticket.
2 These are my pens.
  _____
3 Are those your photos?
  _____
4 Those are the bicycles.
  _____
5 Are these the dogs?
  _____
6 These are the bottles.
  _____
7 Those are my bags.
  _____
8 Are these her combs?
  _____

8

5 Singular and plural nouns

Complete the chart.

Singular	Plural
address	addresses
party	
	visitors
copy	
	people
boy	
	photos
watch	
	cities
lunch	
	families
film	
	buildings

6 Singular and plural nouns

Write *s* where possible.

1 my thing*s*
2 my surname
3 my friend
4 the country
5 a bottle of water
6 a packet of tissue
7 our name
8 my key
9 the beach
10 the city

7 Prepositions of place

Complete with *in, on, next to* or *near*.

1 Brighton is .... England.
2 The Royal Pavilion is very .... the beach.
3 The school isn't in the city centre – it's .... the centre, about one kilometre away.
4 Mexico is .... the USA.
5 This is a photo of me standing .... a mountain. The view from the top is amazing.
6 Brussels is .... the centre of Belgium.
7 This exercise is .... page 9.
8 Page 9 is .... page 8.

8 Vocabulary

Write the numbers in words. Then write the next three numbers.

a 21, 24, 27 *twenty-one, twenty-four, twenty-seven, thirty, thirty-three, thirty-six*
b 15, 20, 25
c 24, 36, 48
d 99, 88, 77

9 Vocabulary

Write the answers in words.

1 47 + 19 = *sixty-six*
2 65 + 8 =
3 55 + 34 =
4 85 + 6 =
5 49 + 62 =
6 150 + 170 =
7 466 + 410 =
8 4500 + 3200 =
9 5350 + 4000 =
10 7500 + 2500 =

10 Vocabulary

Write these times in words.

1 6.05 *It's five past six.*
2 7.30
3 8.45
4 9.00
5 10.15
6 11.40
7 12.10
8 1.25
9 2.35
10 3.50
11 4.20
12 5.55

11 Pronunciation

Cross out the silent letters in these words.

b~~u~~ilding   school   centre   eighty   listen   half   tonight

> **Extension** Correct the false sentences in exercise 1 in your notebook.

UNIT 1

1 NICE TO MEET YOU

3 When's your birthday?

1 Reading

Read the dialogue. Then complete the sentences.

EMILY   Here's a photo of my family.
TERESA Nice! Who's that man on the left? Is it your father?
EMILY   Yes, he's called Paul. And that's my mother next to Dad. Her name is Sarah.
TERESA And the boy on the right – is he your brother?
EMILY   Yes. His name is Mark. And the two people in the centre are my grandparents, Caroline and James. Dad is their son.
TERESA And your dog – what's its name?
EMILY   Our dog is called Penny.

1 Mark: 'Emily is my _____.'
2 Paul: 'My mother is called _____.'
3 Mark: 'Caroline is my _____.'
4 Emily: 'In the photo, my father is _____ my mother.'
5 Sarah: 'My husband is called _____.'
6 James: 'My son is called _____.'

2 Personal pronouns

Complete with *I, he, she, we, they*.

DAVID (1) _____ 'm David and this is Jake. (2) _____ 's from the USA. Emily and Adam are English. (3) _____ 're from Brighton. Teresa is Spanish and (4) _____ 's from Valencia. Katya is Russian and (5) _____ 's from Moscow. This is Pierre and (6) _____ 's Swiss. Today (7) _____ 're all in the centre of Brighton.

3 Possessive adjectives

Complete the chart.

Personal pronouns	I	you	he	she	it	we	they
Possessive adjectives	*my*						

10

UNIT 1

4 Vocabulary

Put the words in the right order. Then complete the family tree.

1 name my Bart is
   My name is Bart.

2 is this family my

3 is mother my this

4 name is her Marge

5 this is father my

6 Homer name is his

7 sisters are my these

8 are names their and Lisa Maggie

9 this grandfather is my

10 Abe name is his

The Simpson family

```
     Grandmother ——— Grandfather
                 (1)
     Mother ——— Father
(2)              (3)
     |
   Bart      Sister      Sister
              (4)         (5)
```

5 Vocabulary

Complete the sentences about the Simpson family.

1 HOMER   'Abe is my *father*'
2 LISA   'Bart is my ___'
3 MARGE   'Lisa and Maggie are my ___'
4 MAGGIE 'Abe is my ___'
5 HOMER   'Bart is my ___'
6 BART   'Maggie is my ___'
7 MARGE   'Homer is my ___'
8 HOMER   'Marge is my ___'

6 Vocabulary

Number the months in the correct order.

April ☐   August ☐   December ☐
February ☐   January [1]   July ☐
June ☐   March ☐   May ☐
November ☐   October ☐   September ☐

7 Vocabulary

Write these dates in words.

1 21/5   *the twenty-first of May*
2 9/7
3 16/6
4 2/11
5 4/3
6 30/8
7 8/2
8 12/9
9 1/4
10 26/10
11 3/12
12 14/1

8 Pronunciation

Mark the stressed syllable. Which word is different?

■
birthday   brother   daughter   family   father
photo   February   sister   today   twentieth

> **Extension** What are the names of the people in your family? When are their birthdays? Write five sentences in your notebook.
>
> *My mother is called Sarah. Her birthday is on the second of March.*

1 NICE TO MEET YOU

4 Integrated Skills Personal information

1 Reading

Read the information about Emily and Adam. Then write questions for the answers below.

NFI WELCOME TO THE NEW FRIENDS INTERNATIONAL WEBSITE

Home
New Friends International
Exchanges
Programme
Photos
Noticeboard
Chatroom

Hello, everyone. I'm Emily Fry and I'm from Brighton in England. I'm 14 years old and my birthday is on 25th January. My favourite singer is Pink.

Hi there! My name is Adam Campbell and I'm English. I'm from Lewes near Brighton and I'm 15 years old. My birthday is on 10th August. My favourite singer is Alicia Keys.

Emily

1 _What's her surname?_
   Fry.
2 _____
   She's English.
3 _____
   Brighton in England.
4 _____
   Fourteen.
5 _____
   The twenty-fifth of January.
6 _____
   Pink.

Adam

1 _____
   Campbell.
2 _____
   He's English.
3 _____
   Lewes near Brighton.
4 _____
   Fifteen.
5 _____
   The tenth of August.
6 _____
   Alicia Keys.

2 Writing

Write information about yourself for a website. Use the texts about Emily and Adam to help you.

3 Crossword

Complete the crossword.

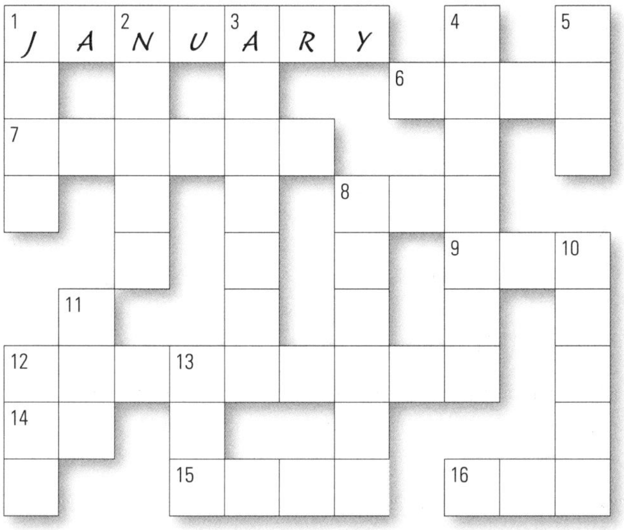

1 J	2 A	3 N	U	A	R	Y		4		5	

(crossword grid)

Across →

1 The first month of the year. (7)
6 Opposite of *false*. (4)
7 95 = … - five (6)
8 'Are you American?' – 'No, I'm …' (3)
9 … old are you? (3)
12 The ninth month of the year. (9)
14 The Royal Pavilion is … the map of Brighton. (2)
15 My sister is … there. (4)
16 Here … your keys. (3)

Down ↓

1 The sixth month of the year. (4)
2 *I* is the … letter of the alphabet. (5)
3 *a* is called the indefinite … (7)
4 Opposite of *sister*. (7)
5 Opposite of *no*. (3)
8 Twenty thousand is a very big … (6)
10 … are you from? (5)
11 What's this in English? (3)
12 Masculine of *daughter*. (3)
13 22 = twenty-… (3)

UNIT 1

LEARNER INDEPENDENCE

Classroom English

Match questions 1–5 with answers a–e.

1 What's  in English?   [d]

2 How do you spell ?   ☐

3 What does *bottle* mean?   ☐

4 How do you pronounce ?   ☐

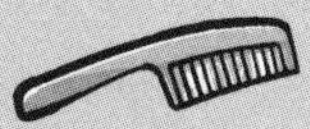

5 What's this called?   ☐

a C-A-L-C-U-L-A-T-O-R
b a wallet
c /kəʊm/ – like *Rome*.
d ticket
e (bottle)

Extensive reading

Read *Blue Fins*. Is it about a shark or a dolphin?

Blue Fins
Sarah Axten

Rick and Jen are on the beach in Australia. The sky and sea are blue and it is hot. Everybody is happy. Then … 'Shark! Quick! Get out of the water!'

1 NICE TO MEET YOU

Inspiration EXTRA!

REVISION

Welcome!

Complete the questions with *What*, *Where*, *Who*. Then look at pages 6–7 of the Student's Book and answer them.

1 _Who_ is from the USA?
   Jake

2 _____ is Teresa from?

3 _____ is the name of the Russian girl?

4 _____ are the names of the English students?

5 _____ isn't a student?

LESSON 1

Look at the pictures and write sentences with *this* or *that*.

1 *This is my ID card.*

2 *That is my pen.*

3

4

5   6

LESSON 2

Draw the hands on the clocks.

1 ten past seven   2 half past four

3 quarter to ten   4 six o'clock

5 twenty past two   6 five to twelve

LESSON 3

Complete the sentences about Emily's family.

```
      Caroline ——— James
   Sarah ——— Paul
         |
    Mark   Emily
```

1 SARAH 'Paul is my _____.'
2 PAUL   'Mark is my _____.'
3 MARK   'Emily is my _____.'
4 EMILY 'Mark is my _____.'
5 PAUL   'Caroline is my _____.'
6 JAMES 'Caroline is my _____.'
7 EMILY 'Caroline is my _____.'
8 MARK   'James is my _____.'
9 SARAH 'Emily is my _____.'
10 EMILY 'Paul is my _____.'

LESSON 4

Complete the questions with *How*, *What*, *When*, *Where*, *Who*. Then read the information about Jake and answer them.

1 _____ is Jake from?

2 _____ is his surname?

3 _____ is his nationality?

4 _____ is his birthday?

5 _____ old is he?

6 _____ is his favourite singer?

> I'm Jake Turner and I'm from Washington in the USA. I'm 14 years old and my birthday is on 11th March. My favourite singer is Jay-Z.

Spelling

Complete these words from Unit 1.

1 be _a_ utiful   2 b___ilding   3 p___otograph   4 cent___e
5 dau___hter   6 e___ght   7 favo___rite   8 fr___end
9 mount___in   10 q___arter

Brainteaser

Mississippi is a very long word. How do you spell it?

Answer on page 29.

UNIT 1

EXTENSION

Welcome!

Look at pages 6–7 of the Student's Book and complete the sentences with *is(n't)* or *are(n't)*.

1 Her name ___is___ Teresa and she _____ from Spain.
2 _____ Emily and Adam at school in Washington? No, they _____.
3 Emily and Adam _____ at school in Washington. They _____ at school in Brighton.
4 We _____ pleased to be here. It's great!
5 My name _____ David Ward and I'm a teacher at Brighton High School.
6 His name _____ Jake. He _____ English – he _____ from the USA.

LESSON 1

Number the sentences in the right order to make a dialogue.

a EMILY Oh, I see. My surname is Fry. ☐
b PIERRE Dubois. It's a French name. ☐
c EMILY Sorry? Pierre what? ☐
d PIERRE Hi, Emily! I'm Pierre Dubois. ☐ *1*
e EMILY F-R-Y. ☐
f PIERRE How do you spell it? ☐

Now write a similar dialogue between you and Katya Petrova in your notebook.

LESSON 2

Correct these sentences.

1 These are my bag.
   These are my bags.
2 Are that your keys?
3 What time is he?
4 It's two clock.
5 How old are it?
6 It's 200 year old.

LESSON 3

Write these important dates in words.

1 Christmas Day (25/12)
   the twenty-fifth of December
2 New Year's Day (1/1)
3 World Water Day (22/3)
4 International Day of Families (15/5)
5 International Youth Day (12/8)

Write three more important dates in words.

LESSON 4

Look at the information about Jake on page 14. Write similar information about two of your friends in your notebook.

Web watch

To find out more about buildings like the temple at Abu Simbel and the Taj Mahal, go to www.wonderclub.com/ForgottenMap.html and click on the map.

Spelling

Correct the spelling of these words from Unit 1 by doubling one letter in each word.

1 a*d*dress 2 bok 3 botle 4 gues 5 pasport
6 sory 7 spel 8 thirten 9 umbrela 10 walet

Brainteaser

What has a neck, but no head?

Answer on page 29.

1 Culture

Countries around the world

The British Isles

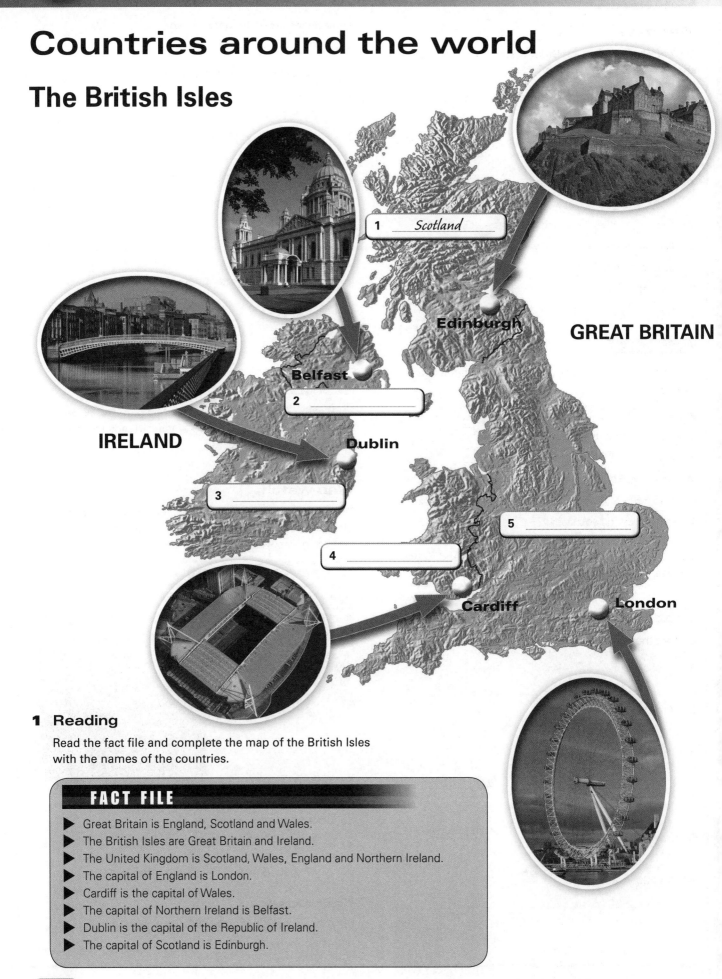

1 Reading

Read the fact file and complete the map of the British Isles with the names of the countries.

FACT FILE

- Great Britain is England, Scotland and Wales.
- The British Isles are Great Britain and Ireland.
- The United Kingdom is Scotland, Wales, England and Northern Ireland.
- The capital of England is London.
- Cardiff is the capital of Wales.
- The capital of Northern Ireland is Belfast.
- Dublin is the capital of the Republic of Ireland.
- The capital of Scotland is Edinburgh.

POPULATION AND LANGUAGES

There are 61,800,000 people in the United Kingdom and the population of England is 51,500,000. English is the main language in England, but there are also speakers of over 180 other languages!

The population of Scotland is 5,200,000. The main languages are English and Scots Gaelic (60,000 speakers). In Wales the first language is English, but there are 750,000 speakers of Welsh. The population of Wales is 3,000,000. The two main languages in Ireland are English and Irish Gaelic. The population of Northern Ireland is 1,789,000 and the population of the Republic of Ireland is 4,500,000.

2 Reading

Read *Population and languages* and complete the chart.

ENGLAND	
Capital	London
Population	51,500,000
Languages	English and over 180 other languages
SCOTLAND	
Capital	
Population	
Languages	
WALES	
Capital	
Population	
Languages	
NORTHERN IRELAND	
Capital	
Population	
Languages	
REPUBLIC OF IRELAND	
Capital	
Population	
Languages	

3 Vocabulary

Match the numbers in list A with the words in list B.

A		B	
a	180	1	fifty-one million, five hundred thousand
b	60,000	2	one hundred and eighty
c	750,000	3	five million, two hundred thousand
d	1,789,000	4	sixty thousand
e	3,000,000	5	four million, five hundred thousand
f	4,500,000	6	sixty-one million, eight hundred thousand
g	5,200,000	7	seven hundred and fifty thousand
h	51,500,000	8	three million
i	61,800,000	9	one million, seven hundred and eighty-nine thousand

2.1 21ST CENTURY WORLD
She has a lovely smile

1 Reading

Emily and Adam are at the welcome party. Read the dialogue. Then read the sentences and write *T* (true) or *F* (false).

EMILY Are your mother and father here?
ADAM My mum is. She's next to Mr Ward. She has long blonde hair. And my sister Ruby is over there with two of her friends.
EMILY Which girl is Ruby?
ADAM She has a blue top and curly blonde hair. Are your parents here?
EMILY Yes, they're over there. My mum is the woman with the green bag and my dad is next to her. He has a blue shirt and black trousers.
ADAM Is your brother here?
EMILY No, he isn't. He's at home.
ADAM Who is that over there?
EMILY The girl with the long dark hair and the pink top?
ADAM Yes.
EMILY That's my friend, Sally.

1 The woman next to Mr Ward has short hair. ☐
2 His father isn't at the party. ☐
3 Ruby has a pink top. ☐
4 Adam has a sister. ☐
5 Emily has a brother. He's at home. ☐
6 Sally has long blonde hair. ☐

2 *have*: affirmative

Complete with *have* or *has*.

1 I _____ three brothers.
2 You _____ a great bag.
3 She _____ a nice sister.
4 He _____ brown eyes.
5 It _____ five colours.
6 We _____ a new teacher.
7 They _____ blue tops.

3 *have*: affirmative

Look at the pictures and write sentences with *have* or *has*.

1 *Emily has a mobile phone.*
2 _____
3 _____
4 _____
5 _____
6 _____

4 Vocabulary

Complete with *a* or *a pair of*.

1 _____ jacket
2 _____ shoes
3 _____ pullover
4 _____ jeans
5 _____ shirt
6 _____ cap
7 _____ trainers
8 _____ trousers

5 Vocabulary

Look at page 24 of the Student's Book. Match the countries with the descriptions of their flags.

> India   Puerto Rico   Japan   Germany   South Africa

1 This country has a black, red and yellow flag.
   ....

2 This country has a white flag with a red circle.
   ....

3 This country has an orange, white and green flag. It has a dark blue wheel in the centre.
   ....

4 This country has a black, green, yellow, red, white and blue flag.
   ....

5 This country has a red, white and blue flag.
   ....

Draw the flag of your country and complete the sentence.

My country has a/an .... flag.

6 Vocabulary

Look at the photos on page 24 of the Student's Book and complete the sentences with words for colours.

1 Laxmi has a *red* sari.
2 Daniel has .... shorts.
3 Kumiko has a .... T-shirt.
4 Pedro and Felipe have .... shirts and .... trousers.
5 Hanna has .... hair and a .... top.
6 Daniel has .... socks and .... shoes.
7 Pedro has a .... hat.
8 Kumiko has .... hair.

7 Crossword

Look at the pictures (1–8) of the clothes below. Complete the crossword and find the missing word ↓.

8 Pronunciation

Do they rhyme (✓) or not (✗)?

1 blue   shoe   ✓
2 no   to   ☐
3 two   you   ☐
4 brown   phone   ☐
5 shirt   skirt   ☐
6 are   pair   ☐
7 hair   there   ☐
8 eye   my   ☐
9 white   right   ☐
10 grey   day   ☐

9 Pronunciation

Mark the stressed syllable. Which word is different?

■
colour   lovely   umbrella   orange   jacket   mobile

pullover   purple   trainers   trousers   yellow

> **Extension** Write five sentences in your notebook describing yourself, your clothes and the things you have.

2 21ST CENTURY WORLD

2 I can play the guitar

1 Reading

Read the dialogue. Then complete the sentences.

PIERRE   What sports can you play, Adam?
ADAM   I can play tennis.
PIERRE   Oh, I can play tennis, too. Can you ski?
ADAM   No, I can't. Can you?
PIERRE   Yes, I can.
ADAM   Can you ride a horse?
PIERRE   No, I can't, but I can ride a bicycle.
ADAM   How many languages can you speak?
PIERRE   I can speak English, French, German and Italian. How about you?
ADAM   I can speak English, of course, and French. I can speak a little Russian, too.
PIERRE   Oh, I can't speak Russian.

1 Adam can play tennis, but he _____ ski.
2 Pierre can play tennis and he can _____.
3 Pierre can't ride a horse, but he can ride a _____.
4 _____ can speak four languages.
5 Pierre can't speak _____.
6 Adam can speak English, _____ and _____.

2 can and can't

Write sentences.

1 Emily/tell jokes ✓ /remember people's names ✗
   Emily can tell jokes, but she can't remember people's names.

2 Emily and Katya/speak French ✓ /speak German ✗

3 Adam/sing ✓ /dance ✗

4 Pierre/draw a picture ✓ /create a web page ✗

5 Teresa/sing ✓ /play an instrument ✗

6 Katya and Jake/make a cake ✗ /make a sandwich ✓

3 can and can't

Write six true sentences.

I	can	play tennis.
		sing.
My teacher		cook a meal.
	can't	iron a shirt.
Horses		burn a CD.
		swim underwater.

1
2
3
4
5
6

4 can and can't

Look at the chart and write questions and answers.

	Adam	Emily
ride a horse	✗	✓
iron a shirt	✓	✗
dance	✗	✓
download music	✓	✗
speak Spanish	✓	✗
swim underwater	✗	✓

1 *Can Adam ride a horse? No, he can't.*
2 *Can he iron a shirt? Yes, he can.*
3
4
5
6
7 *Can Emily*
8 *Can she*
9
10
11
12

5 *can* and *can't*

Look at the chart and write six sentences about what Katya and Jake can and can't do.

	1	2	3	4	5	6
Katya	✓	✓	✗	✓	✓	✗
Jake	✗	✗	✓	✗	✗	✓

1 read — *Katya can read music, but Jake can't.*
2 play
3 play
4 speak
5 sew on
6 remember

6 Linking words: *and, but, or*

Complete with *and, but, or*.

1 Can you read .... listen to music at the same time?
2 I can't find my jacket .... my cap.
3 I can burn a CD, ... I can't create a web page.
4 She can play the saxophone .... the guitar.
5 They can't cook .... sew.
6 He can play the guitar, ... he can't read music.
7 My father can't programme a satnav .... send a text message.
8 She can play tennis, ... she can't ride a horse.

7 Vocabulary

Match the verbs in list A with the words in list B.

	A	B
1	burn	a horse
2	cook	a CD
3	iron	a joke
4	programme	a language
5	ride	a meal
6	lift	a shirt
7	speak	20 kilos
8	tell	a satnav

8 Spelling

The same letter is missing in each line. Write the complete words.

1 cok   jke   peple
    cook
2 gitar   langage   qestion
3 liht   sin   proramme
4 instument   punctue   undewater
5 plac   crate   hors
6 fantasic   swich   wach

9 Vocabulary

Complete with these words.

> behind   dear   draw   light   lots
> mind   nice   questions   this   you

1 Never .... !
2 What's .... ?
3 Oh ....
4 It's really ....
5 Any .... ?
6 Can I help .... with anything?
7 Can you .... a picture?
8 I can't find the .... switch.
9 It's .... the door.
10 We can sing in .... of languages.

10 Pronunciation

Complete the chart with these words.

> ~~anything~~   ~~fantastic~~   instrument   piano   pullover
> bicycle   remember   saxophone   umbrella

■ ■ ■	■ ■ ■
anything	*fantastic*

> **Extension** Write five sentences about things you can and can't do in your notebook.

2.3 21ST CENTURY WORLD
Keep still

1 Reading

Read the dialogue. Then read the sentences and write *T* (true) or *F* (false).

EMILY Do you want to see my photos from the welcome party? They're on my phone.
TERESA Yes, please. Oh, look, there's a lovely one of us.
EMILY Do you want to send it to your mum?
TERESA Can we do that from your phone?
EMILY Yes, of course. We can send it in an email or a multimedia message.
TERESA Really? Can you show me how?
EMILY Sure. First, choose the picture you want and touch it with your finger.
TERESA Right.
EMILY OK, now, you see that square with the arrow at the bottom of the screen?
TERESA Yes.
EMILY Touch that. OK, now you can choose email or multimedia message. Do you know the email address?
TERESA Yes.
EMILY Right, well, select 'Email'. That's right – touch it with your finger and then type her address in the box.
TERESA OK. Now what?
EMILY Touch 'Send' at the top.
TERESA Right. Is that it?
EMILY Yes, it's sending it now.
TERESA Wow! That's really easy.

1 The photos of the welcome party are on a camera. ☐
2 There is a good photo of Teresa and Emily. ☐
3 Teresa sends the photo to her teacher. ☐
4 Emily can send photos by email from her phone. ☐
5 Teresa doesn't know the email address. ☐
6 There is something wrong with the phone. ☐

2 Imperatives

Look at the pictures and complete.

Don't move.   Press OK.   Come here.
Don't run.   ~~Smile.~~   Don't forget your jacket.

1 Smile.
2
3
4
5
6

3 Imperatives

Rewrite these requests using the imperative.

1 Can you speak English, please?
   Speak English.
2 Please don't be late.
   _____

3 Can you give him the message, please?
   _____
4 Please don't use my phone.
   _____

UNIT 2

4 Imperatives

Complete with these verbs. Use *don't* where necessary.

> ~~ask~~   be   forget   go   help
> keep   select   tell   use

1 *Don't ask* me my age!
2 Phone me tomorrow – _____ my number!
3 _____ to Menu and _____ Audio.
4 _____ late for the welcome party.
5 _____ me, please. I can't programme the satnav.
6 _____ your mobile for international calls. It's really expensive.
7 _____ me his name. I can't remember it.
8 _____ still. Don't move around.

5 Definite article

Complete with *the* where necessary.

1 *The* capital of _____ Spain is Madrid.
2 He plays _____ piano.
3 _____ main language of _____ Mexico is _____ Spanish.
4 Can you download music from _____ Internet?
5 What is _____ phone number of the school?
6 What's wrong with your webcam? _____ picture isn't very good.
7 *A* is _____ first letter of _____ alphabet.
8 _____ River Nile is in _____ Egypt.

6 Definite article

Correct these sentences by adding *the*.

1 Now enter phone number.
   Now enter the phone number.
2 Here's phone and that's number.
3 Dial area code.
4 International code for Switzerland is 0041.
5 Area code for Geneva is 022.
6 Emily is on right in photo.

7 Vocabulary

Match the words in list A with the words in list B to make eight compound words. Then write the words.

	A	B	
1	area	camera	1 *area code*
2	boy	code	2
3	digital	friend	3
4	light	message	4
5	mobile	cam	5
6	text	phone	6
7	lap	switch	7
8	web	top	8

8 Vocabulary

Match the verbs in list A with the words in list B.

	A	B
1	move	a call
2	dial	a name
3	make	a number
4	keep	a picture
5	spell	around
6	take	still

9 Writing

Write this text message in full in your notebook.

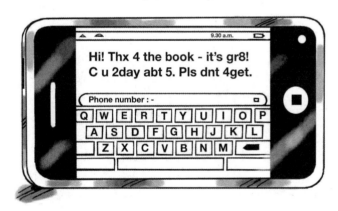

10 Pronunciation

Do they rhyme (✓) or not (✗)?

1 course   horse   ✓
2 dial   smile   □
3 move   love   □
4 hi   bye   □
5 late   great   □
6 send   friend □
7 phone   one   □
8 now   know   □

> **Extension** In your notebook, write sentences using the imperative to tell someone how to use your mobile phone/computer/MP3 player/camera, etc.

23

2.4 21ST CENTURY WORLD
Integrated Skills Favourite band

1 Reading

Read and complete with these words.

| hair | its | film | has | blonde | black | special | jacket | have | songs |

TOP OF THE POP STARS

Above the Noise by McFly is my favourite album. The band (**1**) _____ four members and (**2**) _____ name comes from Marty McFly – the main character in the *Back to the Future* films.

In the photo, Harry Judd is on the left. He has a (**3**) _____ top and black trousers. Tom Fletcher and Dougie Poynter (in the centre) have short (**4**) _____ hair and jeans. Danny Jones is next to Dougie and he has short black (**5**) _____. He has black jeans and a cream (**6**) _____. And they all (**7**) _____ really nice eyes.

Two (**8**) _____ things about the band: they are the youngest band to have a number 1 album in the UK, and you can see them in a (**9**) _____ with Lindsay Lohan called *Just My Luck*. All the (**10**) _____ on the film soundtrack are also by McFly.

2 Writing

Look at the photo of the Black Eyed Peas on pages 30–31 of the Student's Book. Write a description of the members of the band (hair and clothes). You can use the text about McFly to help you.

3 Crossword

Complete the crossword.

Across →

1. Adam has three text ... on his mobile. (8)
7. Opposite of *yes*. (2)
8. Tom Fletcher and Dougie Poynter ... blonde hair. (4)
9. Opposite of *girl*. (3)
11. Washington is ... the USA. (2)
12. Can you come over ...? (4)
14. Can I send the photo ... my mum? (2)
15. I'm = I ... (2)
16. Laxmi has brown ... (4)
19. Excuse ... (2)
21. ... , two, three. (3)
22. The international ... for Switzerland is 0041. (4)
23. Can you ... a satnav? (9)

Down ↓

1. Adam has a new ... phone. (6)
2. How do you ... this word? (3)
3. ... questions? (3)
4. ... to Menu and select Audio. (2)
5. Pedro has a white ... (5)
6. Can you ... people's names? (8)
10. Can you sew ... a button? (2)
12. Sorry, you can't borrow my pen. It's at ... (4)
13. We're very pleased to ... here. (2)
17. There are twelve months in a ... (4)
18. We can sing a ... in English. (4)
20. LUV = ... (4)

LEARNER INDEPENDENCE

Classroom English

Match questions 1–5 with answers a–e.

1. Excuse me. Can you help me, please?
2. Please can I borrow your book?
3. Excuse me. What's this in English?
4. Please can I leave the room?
5. Excuse me. How do you say this word?

a. Notebook.
b. Yes, of course you can. Please close the door.
c. /kɑːnt/
d. No, I'm sorry. You can't today, but you can tomorrow.
e. Yes, of course. What's the problem?

Extensive reading

Read *L.A. Detective*. Write a description (hair and clothes) of Len and Carmen.

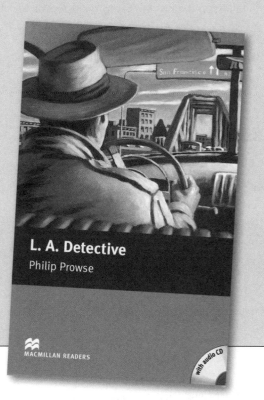

'My name is Lenny Samuel. My friends call me Len. I'm a detective. I work in Los Angeles. I'm an L.A. detective.'

2 21st CENTURY WORLD

Inspiration EXTRA!

REVISION

LESSON 1

Complete with *has* or *have*.

1 Tara Tress .... blonde hair.
2 We .... long hair.
3 I .... brown hair.
4 All three boys .... blue jeans.
5 We .... black and white trainers.
6 Mr Ward .... a brown jacket.
7 She .... a yellow top.
8 I .... a digital camera.
9 You .... your address book with you.
10 Teresa .... three pairs of jeans.

Put the letters in the right order to make words for clothes.

1 thris   *shirt*   5 loverlup ....
2 etkcaj ....   6 sretnair ....
3 hoses ....   7 pac ....
4 triks ....   8 snaje ....

LESSON 2

Write questions and answers.

1 Teresa can play the saxophone. ✗
  Can Teresa play the saxophone? No, she can't.
2 Teresa can sing. ✓
3 Emily can play the guitar. ✓
4 Emily can speak German. ✗
5 Katya can find her trainers. ✗
6 Adam can send a text message. ✓
7 Katya can ride a horse. ✓
8 Adam can dance. ✗
9 Pierre can cook a meal. ✓

LESSON 3

Put the words in the right order to make imperative sentences.

1 to picture the send your mum
  Send the picture to your mum.
2 of picture Pierre take a
3 code international the dial
4 code forget the area don't
5 friend later phone your
6 house to come eight my at
7 use mobile your don't

LESSON 4

Write questions for these answers about Linkin Park.

1 *What's your favourite band?*
  Linkin Park.
2 ....
  Six.
3 ....
  California in the USA.
4 ....
  Leave Out All the Rest.
5 ....
  www.linkinpark.com

Spelling

Complete these words from Unit 2.

1 bla__k   2 clot__es   3 fanta__tic   4 g__itar
5 lig__t   6 mes__age   7 num__er   8 pict__re
9 p__rple 10 remem__er 11 tro__sers 12 yel__ow

Brainteaser

What word has twenty-six letters?

Answer on page 29.

26

UNIT 2

EXTENSION

LESSON 1

Match questions 1–6 with answers a–f.

1. Are your brother and sister here? ☐
2. Can I borrow your pullover? ☐
3. Can you come over here? ☐
4. What about your family? ☐
5. What's wrong with your webcam? ☐
6. Which boy is Jake? ☐

a. He has a cap and black jeans.
b. I have two sisters.
c. The picture isn't very good.
d. My brother is.
e. No, I'm sorry. It's at home.
f. Yes, of course I can.

LESSON 2

Correct the questions. Then answer them for you.

1. You can sing and dance at the same time?
   Can you sing and dance at the same time?

2. Can you speak the French or German?

3. Can you play instrument?

4. Can you remember people's name?

5. Can you makes a cake or a sandwich?

6. Can you sew on button?

7. You can answer the Life Skills Questionnaire?

8. Can you to run five kilometres?

LESSON 3

Choose the correct words to complete the instructions.

How to take and send a picture on a camera phone.
1. Enter / **Go** to 'Menu'.
2. Keep / Select 'Camera'.
3. Press / Keep **the phone still**.
4. Press / Go 'OK'.
5. Presses / Press 'Select'.
6. Select / Go 'Send via multimedia'.
7. Enter / Keep **the phone number**.
8. Press / See 'Send'.

LESSON 4

Write a paragraph about your favourite singer in your notebook.

Web watch

Go to www.bbc.co.uk/radio1/chart/singles
Which bands and singers are in the top 40 this week?

Spelling

Read and complete these words from Unit 2.

- We pronounce the first letter of the alphabet /eɪ/.
- When we hear the sound /eɪ/ in the middle of a word, the usual spelling is *a*-consonant-*e*:
  cake   date   (**1**) ma_*k*_e   (**2**) na......e   (**3**) pla......e
  (**4**) ta......e
- The sound /eɪ/ at the end of a word is often spelt *ay*:
  Monday   (**5**) pl............   (**6**) s............   (**7**) tod............
  But note: *they*.

Brainteaser

When is it correct to say *I is ...*?

Answer on page 29.

REVIEW
Units 1–2

1 Read and complete. For each number 1–10, choose word A, B or C.

MR WARD Hello, and now it's time for our welcome party quiz! And Teresa __1__ here to answer the questions. OK, Teresa? Your questions are about clothes and colours. First, clothes. OK? Number one: what *C* has three letters?
TERESA __2__.
MR WARD Yes! What *J* __3__ five letters?
TERESA Jeans.
MR WARD That's right. What *T* has eight letters?
TERESA __4__.
MR WARD Correct. What *S* has four letters?
TERESA I can't __5__.
MR WARD The second __6__ is *H*.
TERESA Shoe!
MR WARD Yes! And the last clothes question. What *S* has five letters?
TERESA __7__.
MR WARD And now colours. What two *B*s have five letters?
TERESA Black __8__ brown.
MR WARD Correct. And now can you tell me what *P* has six letters?
TERESA __9__.
MR WARD And now the last colours question. What *Y* has six letters?
TERESA Yellow.
MR WARD That's eight correct __10__. Fantastic!

1	A are	(B is)	C has
2	A Can	B Cap	C Cup
3	A has	B have	C is
4	A tissues	B trainer	C trousers
5	A forget	B know	C remember
6	A letter	B number	C word
7	A Shirt	B Smile	C Sweet
8	A and	B but	C or
9	A People	B Purple	C Pink
10	A answers	B letters	C questions

2 Read the definitions and complete the words.

1 You look at this to check the time.   w _a_ _t_ _c_ _h_
2 You look at this to find a place.   m _ _
3 You take photos with this.   c _ _ _ _
4 You write with this.   p _ _
5 You read this.   b _
6 You do your hair with this.   c _ _
7 You can send text messages with this.   m _ _ _ _ _ _
8 This is a musical instrument.   g _ _ _ _

28

3 Complete the dialogues. Choose A, B or C.

1 What's this called?
A His name is David.
B You have a message.
C (It's a calculator.)

2 What time is it?
A It's half past seven.
B It's tonight.
C It's a beautiful day.

3 Can you play the piano?
A Yes, you can.
B Yes, I can.
C It's at home.

4 Can I help you?
A I can't remember.
B Yes, I can't open the door.
C No, I'm sorry.

5 Can I see the photos?
A Here you are.
B It's here.
C Never mind.

4 Find the odd word.

1 pavilion   house   (river)   temple
2 road   school   student   teacher
3 brother   father   girlfriend   mother
4 in   near   on   or
5 jacket   jeans   pullover   shirt
6 band   guitar   piano   saxophone
7 lift   run   swim   walk
8 menu   message   number   parent

Answers to Brainteasers

UNIT 1
Revision I-T
Extension A bottle.

UNIT 2
Revision Alphabet.
Extension I is the ninth letter of the alphabet.

LEARNER INDEPENDENCE
SELF ASSESSMENT

1 Draw this chart in your notebook. How many words can you write in each category?

More than 10? Good!   *More than 12?* Very good!
More than 15? Excellent!

Family	
Clothes	
Colours	
Music	

2 Put the words in order to make expressions from the phrasebooks in Lesson 4 in Units 1 and 2.

1 I oh see
   Oh, I see.

2 very you thank much

3 wrong something there's

4 you of course can yes

5 a thanks lot

6 cool really it's

Check your answers.
6/6 Excellent!   *4/6* Very good!   *2/6* Try again!

My learning diary
In Units 1 and 2:

My favourite topic is

My favourite picture is

The three lessons I like most are

My favourite activity or exercise is

Something I don't understand is

Something I want to learn more about is

3 LIFESTYLE

1 I really don't like octopus

1 Reading

Read *Pizza puzzle*. Then match the pizzas with the girls.

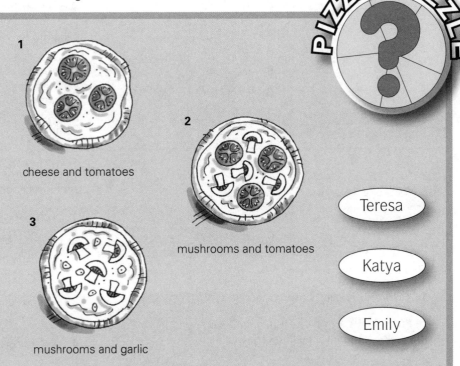

Teresa, Emily and Katya are at a pizza restaurant. They all want different things on their pizza. One girl likes mushrooms and tomatoes, but she doesn't like garlic or cheese. One girl likes mushrooms and garlic, but she doesn't like tomatoes. The third girl doesn't like mushrooms or garlic, but she likes tomatoes and cheese. Emily isn't the girl who doesn't like tomatoes. Katya doesn't like garlic or cheese.

1 cheese and tomatoes
2 mushrooms and tomatoes
3 mushrooms and garlic

Teresa
Katya
Emily

2 Present simple: affirmative

Write sentences using the present simple.

1 Ruby and Adam/live/in a cottage
   Ruby and Adam live in a cottage.
2 Pierre/live/in a flat
3 Diana/have/two children
4 we/want/to talk to you
5 Ruby/like/eggs for breakfast
6 you/hate/cucumber
7 the chickens/live/in the garden
8 I/love/your jeans

3 Present simple: affirmative

Complete with the present simple form of these verbs.

| hate | have | hope | like | ~~live~~ | play | speak | want |

1 They *live* in the city centre.
2 Emily _____ French.
3 I _____ to eat something now – I'm really hungry!
4 She doesn't like chocolate – she _____ it.
5 Pierre _____ everything except octopus.
6 Katya _____ a sister called Anna.
7 Emily _____ the saxophone.
8 I _____ you aren't angry.

4 Present simple: affirmative and negative

Choose the correct word(s) to complete the sentences.

1 Teresa **play** / **doesn't play** an instrument.
2 Fish **live** / **don't live** in water.
3 You **use** / **doesn't use** a mobile phone to send a message.
4 They **speak** / **don't speak** Spanish in China.
5 Flats **has** / **don't have** gardens.
6 We **want** / **doesn't want** to have dinner now.

UNIT 3

5 Present simple: affirmative and negative

Correct these sentences.

1 Adam lives in Brighton. (Lewes)
   Adam doesn't live in Brighton. He lives in Lewes.

2 Teresa likes Lady Gaga. (Rihanna)

3 He wants to have fish. (pizza)

4 Pierre and his parents have a house. (flat)

5 Ruby has a red top. (blue top)

6 Adam likes tomatoes. (mushrooms)

7 Ruby and Adam live in a flat. (cottage)

8 We want to see the fish. (chickens)

6 Present simple: affirmative and negative

Write sentences.

1 Pierre/like/eggs ✓/octopus ✗
   Pierre likes eggs, but he doesn't like octopus.

2 Ruby/eat/chocolate ✓/bananas ✗

3 Emily/speak/Italian ✓/German ✗

4 Pierre/play/tennis ✓/football ✗

5 Teresa and Emily/hate/Robbie Williams ✓/Madonna ✗

7 Vocabulary

Find 12 words for food in the word square.

A	C	U	C	U	M	B	E	R	M
Y	H	B	R	N	O	E	G	O	E
T	O	A	C	S	C	E	G	D	N
O	C	N	A	G	T	T	S	W	I
M	O	A	R	A	O	F	B	O	R
A	L	N	R	R	P	I	Z	Z	A
T	A	A	O	L	U	S	D	J	B
O	T	W	T	I	S	H	E	U	Y
M	E	Y	G	C	H	E	E	S	E
O	M	U	S	H	R	O	O	M	P

8 Vocabulary

Answer the questions.

Which food is …

1 orange?   c*arrots*
2 brown?   c
3 white?   g
                   m
4 green?   c
5 grey?   f
6 pink?   o
7 yellow?   b
                   c
8 red?   t
9 yellow and red? p
10 yellow and white? e

9 Pronunciation

Mark the stressed syllable.

■

banana   breakfast   carrot   chicken
chocolate   cottage   cucumber   garden
garlic   mushroom   octopus   tomato

> **Extension** Write three sentences about food you like in your notebook.

31

3 LIFESTYLE

2 Does she study in the evening?

1 Reading

Read *My best friend*. Then read the sentences and write *T* (true) or *F* (false).

MY BEST FRIEND

14-year-old Annabel Parker gets up at 6.30 and goes for a walk with Sunny. Then she has breakfast and gets her books ready for school. She puts on her coat and says goodbye to her mum and her brother. Her school is two kilometres from her home. Annabel walks there with Sunny. They arrive at her school at 8.30. Annabel says hello to her friends, takes off her coat and goes to her classroom. Sunny goes with her. Her first lesson is at 9.00 and Sunny sits on the floor next to her desk. Annabel is blind – she can't see. Sunny is her guide dog. He helps her walk from her home to her school. He crosses the road when there are no cars. He takes her from the classroom to the lunch room and then to the gym. The last lesson of the day is history. Annabel likes history. It ends at 3.30. The bell rings and Annabel puts her books in her bag. Then she and Sunny walk home together.

1 Annabel has a brother called Sunny. ☐
2 Annabel has breakfast before she goes for a walk with Sunny. ☐
3 Sunny goes to school with Annabel. ☐
4 Sunny sits outside the classroom in lessons. ☐
5 Sunny helps Annabel cross roads and find her way. ☐
6 Annabel takes the bus home from school. ☐

2 Present simple: questions and short answers

Complete the questions and short answers.

RUBY (1) *Do you live* (live) in the city centre?
PIERRE (2) Yes, *I do.*
RUBY (3) .... (have) a garden?
PIERRE (4) No, ...
RUBY (5) .... (eat) eggs?
PIERRE (6) Yes, ...
RUBY (7) .... (want) to talk to Adam?
PIERRE (8) No, ...
RUBY (9) .... (love) fish?
PIERRE (10) Yes, ...
RUBY (11) .... (like) octopus.
PIERRE (12) No, ...

3 Present simple: questions

Write questions. Then look at Adam's timetable on page 41 of the Student's Book and answer them.

1 when/Adam/have PE
When does Adam have PE? On Wednesday at 14.10.
2 when/lessons/start in the morning
....
3 what/Adam/have on Monday at 11.30
....
4 when/the students/have lunch
....
5 when/lessons/start after lunch
....
6 when/Adam/have computer studies
....

4 Prepositions of time

Complete with *at, in, on*.

1 .... Friday
2 .... twelve o'clock
3 .... the evening
4 .... night
5 .... Sunday
6 .... 2.10
7 .... the morning
8 .... five past ten
9 .... the afternoon
10 .... 3.50

5 Prepositions of time

Complete with *after, at, before, in, on, from, to*.

Adam starts school (**1**) _____ nine o'clock (**2**) _____ the morning. The first lesson is (**3**) _____ nine (**4**) _____ five past ten, and the second lesson is (**5**) _____ five past ten (**6**) _____ ten past eleven. Break is (**7**) _____ ten past eleven and lessons start again (**8**) _____ half past eleven, (**9**) _____ break. Then there are two more lessons (**10**) _____ lunch. Lunch is (**11**) _____ ten past one (**12**) _____ ten past two. (**13**) _____ lunch, he has one lesson (**14**) _____ the afternoon. (**15**) _____ Wednesday, he has PE (**16**) _____ lunch.

6 Present simple: questions and short answers

Write questions and short answers.

1 Annabel walks to school every day. ✓
   Does Annabel walk to school every day?
   Yes, she does.

2 Annabel plays basketball at break. ✗

3 Annabel has a short break in the morning. ✓

4 They have lots of activities after school. ✗

5 Annabel hates history. ✗

6 You like sport. ✓

7 Annabel and her friends do art after school. ✗

8 Students at your school play sports. ✓

7 Vocabulary

Find words for the seven days of the week in the word square.

W	E	D	N	E	S	D	A	Y
T	H	U	R	S	D	A	Y	X
U	F	K	P	I	B	L	T	M
E	F	R	I	D	A	Y	L	O
S	N	W	J	O	L	D	W	N
D	S	U	N	D	A	Y	E	D
A	B	R	G	O	W	S	P	A
Y	S	A	T	U	R	D	A	Y

8 Vocabulary

Match the words for school subjects with the pictures.

art [3]   computer studies [ ]   English [ ]
French [ ]   geography [ ]   history [ ]
maths [ ]   PE [ ]   science [ ]

9 Pronunciation

Complete the chart with these words.

| ~~blue~~ | ~~but~~ | come | fun | love | lunch |
| one | school | soon | too | up | you |

/uː/ **do**	/ʌ/ **does**
blue	*but*

Extension   Correct the false sentences in exercise 1 in your notebook.

3 LIFESTYLE

3 I never lift weights

1 Reading

Read the text. Then read the sentences and choose the correct words.

Martin goes swimming every morning before breakfast. Then he cycles to school. He plays basketball on Monday, Wednesday and Friday. He plays football on Thursday after school and he goes running on Saturday morning. He doesn't do any sport on Sunday. His sister Anna doesn't like sport. She can't swim and she hates running. She goes shopping every Saturday morning and she goes to the cinema on Saturday evening.

1 Martin **never / sometimes** takes the bus to school.
2 Martin **sometimes / always** cycles to school.
3 Martin **never / often** plays basketball.
4 Martin **always / never** plays football on Wednesday.
5 Anna **sometimes / never** goes swimming or running.
6 Anna **sometimes / always** goes shopping on Saturday.

2 Adverbs of frequency

Rewrite these sentences with the adverb in **bold** in the correct position.

1 Adam is late for school.   **sometimes**
  Adam is sometimes late for school.

2 Emily goes to the gym on Monday.   **usually**

3 Emily goes shopping on Sunday.   **never**

4 Pierre is at the swimming pool on Monday.   **always**

5 Adam plays tennis at the weekend.   **often**

6 Teresa does her homework in the evening.   **usually**

7 Ruby is angry with Adam.   **sometimes**

3 Adverbs of frequency

Look at the chart and write sentences about Jake.

Jake's week		
Monday	🏊	often
Tuesday	🏀	always
Wednesday		sometimes
Thursday		usually
Friday	🏃	usually
Saturday		never
Sunday	🎾	often

1 *He often goes swimming on Monday.*
2
3
4
5
6
7

4 Adverbs of frequency

Look at the chart and write sentences about how often Teresa and Adam do things at the gym.

	Teresa	Adam
lift weights	never	sometimes
ride the exercise bike	usually	always
go on the rowing machine	sometimes	often
use the running machine	often	usually
go to dance classes	always	never

1 *Teresa never lifts weights, but Adam sometimes lifts weights.*
2
3
4
5

5 Adverbs of frequency

Answer the questions using *always, usually, often, sometimes* or *never*.

How often do you …

1 go to bed early?
   I sometimes go to bed early.

2 get up late?

3 stay in bed all day?

4 use email?

5 write letters?

6 help your parents?

7 watch TV in bed?

6 Vocabulary

Match the words in list A with the words in list B to make eight compound words. Then write the words.

	A	B		
1	after	bike	1	*afternoon*
2	computer	court	2	
3	dance	end	3	
4	exercise	game	4	
5	swimming	noon	5	
6	tennis	pool	6	
7	time	routine	7	
8	week	table	8	

7 Vocabulary

Write the opposites.

1 always — *never*
2 day
3 go to bed
4 late
5 before
6 stop

8 Vocabulary

Match these words and phrases with *go* or *play*.

basketball   computer games   dancing
football   the guitar   running   shopping
swimming   tennis   to bed

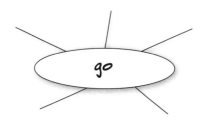

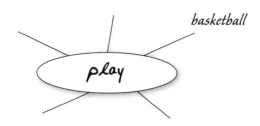
basketball

9 Pronunciation

Do they rhyme (✓) or not (✗)?

1	great	start	✗
2	weight	late	
3	goes	does	
4	run	one	
5	friend	end	
6	gym	time	
7	go	row	
8	learn	burn	

Extension Write six sentences in your notebook about three things that you usually do on holiday and three things that you never do.

> I usually see my grandparents.
> I never do any homework.

3.4 LIFESTYLE
Integrated Skills Personal profiles

1 Reading

Read and complete with these words.

early   classes   loves   goes   always   practises   speaks   have   walls   sees

Roger Federer, born 8th August 1981 (at 8.40am), is an international tennis champion from Switzerland. He says his lucky number is 88 from his birthday (8th August = 8/8). Roger has dark brown hair and brown eyes. He (1) _____ wears a bandana on his head when he plays tennis.

On tournament days, he has a routine – he likes to get everything ready (2) _____. He gets up, has breakfast and (3) _____ on the tennis court. He gets his rackets ready, and puts a banana and another pair of tennis shoes in his tennis bag.

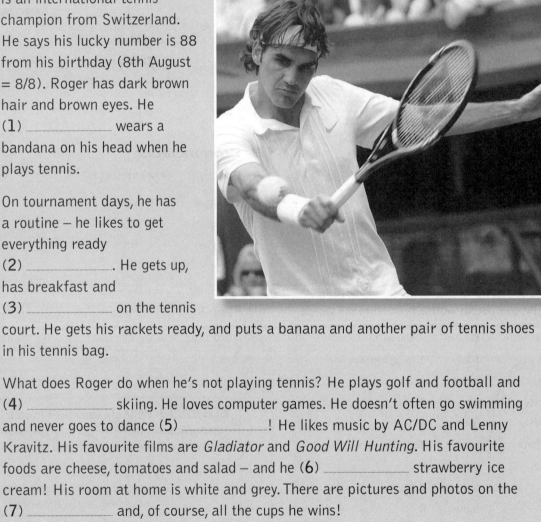

What does Roger do when he's not playing tennis? He plays golf and football and (4) _____ skiing. He loves computer games. He doesn't often go swimming and never goes to dance (5) _____! He likes music by AC/DC and Lenny Kravitz. His favourite films are *Gladiator* and *Good Will Hunting*. His favourite foods are cheese, tomatoes and salad – and he (6) _____ strawberry ice cream! His room at home is white and grey. There are pictures and photos on the (7) _____ and, of course, all the cups he wins!

When it's not a tournament week, Roger usually (8) _____ his family and friends. His wife is called Mirka and they (9) _____ two daughters, Myla and Charlene. He (10) _____ three languages: Swiss German with his Swiss friends, French with his trainer and English with many of the players at tournaments.

UNIT 3

2 Writing

Write a paragraph about Maria Sharapova using these facts.

Maria Sharapova
born 19th April 1987
international tennis champion
from Siberia in Russia
long blonde hair, green eyes
before a tournament usually eats lots of pasta and salad
loves shopping, looking good, being with friends
likes fashion, singing, jazz dancing
favourite film is *Pearl Harbor*
favourite food is Russian food and Italian bread

3 Crossword

Complete the crossword.

Across →
1 Pierre can have fresh eggs for … (9)
5 He … French and German. (6)
6 In the morning. (2)
7 Opposite of *love*. (4)
9 Good friends help … other. (4)
10 The gym Katya goes to is always … in the afternoon. (4)
11 Do you want an … cream? (3)
13 Don't speak to … like that. (2)
14 Adam has his first … from 9 to 10.05. (6)

Down ↓
1 Pierre plays … on Tuesday. (10)
2 Emily goes on the … bike after the running machine. (8)
3 Adam likes … and chips. (4)
4 Adam has 25 lessons on his school … (9)
6 What do you do … lunchtime? (2)
8 Volleyball is … (1, 4)
12 What … your favourite food? (2)
13 '… name is Pierre and I'm Swiss.' (2)

LEARNER INDEPENDENCE

International words

Which of these words from Unit 3 are like words in your language?

banana   cinema   computer   geography
maths   menu   pizza   rock   gym   weekend

Extensive reading

Read *Shooting Stars* and write short descriptions of Matt Lepardi and Claudia Carmen.

Lisa and Alice are on holiday. They are on a plane to Greece. There is a film on the plane. Matt Lepardi and Claudia Carmen are in the film. Matt and Claudia are Lisa and Alice's favourite film stars. Then Lisa sees Matt and Claudia in Greece.

3 LIFESTYLE

Inspiration EXTRA!

REVISION

LESSON 1

Read about the students' likes and dislikes. Then write sentences.

"I like carrots, but I don't like cucumber."

1 *Jake likes carrots, but he doesn't like cucumber.*

"I don't like fish or garlic."

2 ....

"I don't like ice cream, but I like chocolate!"

3 ....

LESSON 2

Write questions and then answer them.

1 Babar Ali/like history
   Does Babar Ali like history? Yes, he does.

2 Chumki Hajra/go to school in the morning

3 Adam/have maths on Wednesday

4 Adam/have a break in the morning

5 you/like history

6 you/have lunch at school

LESSON 3

Write sentences using the adverbs of frequency in **bold**.

1 Jake/go to bed late at the weekend — **usually**

2 Emily/have breakfast in bed on Sunday — **sometimes**

3 Adam and Ruby/watch TV all day — **never**

4 Teresa and Katya/listen to music — **often**

5 Pierre/help in the house — **always**

LESSON 4

Look at the article about Lewis Hamilton on page 44 of the Student's Book and answer the questions.

1 When is his birthday?

2 Does he have brown hair?

3 Where does he live?

4 When does he go running?

5 Does he go to the gym?

6 What kind of food does he like?

7 What is his brother called?

8 What kind of music does he like?

Spelling

Complete these words from Unit 3.

1 car....ot 2 che....se 3 cot....age 4 dif....erent
5 din....er 6 eg.... 7 les....on 8 piz....a 9 run....ing
10 sho....ping 11 sl....ep 12 swim....ing 13 te....nager
14 ten....is 15 vol....eyball 16 we....kend

Brainteaser

Where does Thursday come before Wednesday?

Answer on page 53.

UNIT 3

EXTENSION

LESSON 1

Correct these sentences.

1 She doesn't likes cheese.
   She doesn't like cheese.
2 I speaks French and German.
3 She don't want to talk to me.
4 They doesn't have a garden.
5 He want to have pizza and chips.
6 We really not like octopus.

LESSON 2

Complete with *at*, *in*, *on*, *from* or *to*.

(1) _____ the weekend, I get up (2) _____ eight o'clock and go running (3) _____ eight (4) _____ eight thirty. I have breakfast (5) _____ nine o'clock with my parents. (6) _____ Saturday, I do homework (7) _____ the morning and play football (8) _____ two (9) _____ four o'clock (10) _____ the afternoon. I love dancing and (11) _____ Saturday evening I go dancing (12) _____ eight o'clock. I come home (13) _____ ten o'clock and go to bed (14) _____ eleven. (15) _____ Sunday, we go and see my grandparents for lunch (16) _____ one o'clock. We watch TV (17) _____ the afternoon and come home (18) _____ seven o'clock (19) _____ the evening. And (20) _____ Monday, it's time for school!

LESSON 3

Complete with these adverbs.

| always | usually | often | sometimes | never |
| 100% - 0% |

1 We _____ go swimming at the weekend – nine weekends out of ten.
2 They _____ go running – not every day, but three or four times a week.
3 He _____ goes to dance classes on Wednesday. He never misses a class.
4 She _____ lifts weights because she isn't 16 yet.
5 I _____ go to the gym, but not very often.

LESSON 4

Write a paragraph about your favourite film or sports star in your notebook. Write about these things.

| birthday | where he/she lives | music | food | pets | holidays |

Web watch

Search for 'Lewis Hamilton' and 'Roger Federer' on the Internet and find out more about them. Look up new words in your dictionary and add them to your vocabulary notebook.

Spelling

Read and complete these words from Unit 3.

- We pronounce the ninth letter of the alphabet /aɪ/.
- When we hear the sound /aɪ/ in the middle of a word, the usual spelling is *i*-consonant-*e*:
  bike   (1) i__e   (2) ji__e   (3) qui__e
  (4) ti__e   (5) wri__e

Brainteaser

Which six-letter word for a food in Unit 3 has only three letters?

Answer on page 53.

3 Culture

Take two teenagers ... north and south

Will

I'm 15 and I live with my mum, Susy, and my 12-year-old sister, Carrie. Our flat is near the centre of Bristol, in the west of England.

From Monday to Friday, my alarm clock rings at 6.30am, but I go back to sleep and twenty minutes later I hear my mum say, 'Are you up?' I get up, have a shower and put on my school uniform. Downstairs, I put gel in my hair and put my homework in my bag. Breakfast is two pieces of toast and then I catch the bus to school.

The bell rings at 9am and school starts. We have two lessons, a short break and then four more lessons before lunch. I usually have sandwiches or a hamburger for lunch. After lunch, we have two more lessons (four on Wednesdays) and school ends at 3.30pm. My friends and I have 13 subjects and my favourites are English and music.

Music is a big part of my life. I play the piano and saxophone and have lessons for both of them. I play in the school orchestra and a jazz band. I love sport and play tennis and badminton after school. In the evening, I sometimes play football or go out with my friends and there's always homework – lots of it. At the weekend, it's music, sport, TV and sleep!

Rebecca

I live in Sydney, Australia with my parents and my brothers Brad, 13, and Ryan, 11. I'm 15 and we live in a big house near the sea.

On weekdays, I usually get up at 7.00 and have a shower. I put on my school uniform and have a quick breakfast of eggs, toast and fruit. I leave home at 7.30am and catch the train over the Harbour Bridge to school. I get to school at 8am and talk to my friends or go to the computer room. Lessons start at 8.45 and break is at 10.45 for 20 minutes. Then we have lessons until lunch at 1pm. Classes start after lunch at 1.45pm and school ends at 3pm. My favourite lessons are science and maths.

We have really good lunches at school: sandwiches, ice cream, garlic bread, jaffles (that's the Australian word for toasted sandwiches), rice and cheese. After school, I have a piano lesson and usually go swimming with my friends. In my free time, I watch TV (my favourite programme is *The Simpsons*), read (I love the *Twilight* books) and listen to music. Our summer holiday is in December (your winter) and we go to the Gold Coast in Queensland – it has some really beautiful beaches.

Culture

1 Reading

Read the texts about Will and Rebecca. Then answer the questions.

Who …

1 has two brothers? *Rebecca*
2 lives near the sea? ....
3 gets up at 6.50? ....
4 has a school uniform? ....
5 catches a bus to school? ....
6 starts school at 8.45am? ....
7 likes English? ....
8 has lunch at 1pm? ....
9 has piano lessons? ....
10 plays in a jazz band? ....
11 likes *The Simpsons*? ....
12 plays badminton? ....
13 watches TV? ....
14 goes swimming? ....

2 Vocabulary

Match the words with the pictures.

bell ☐   bread ☐   gel ☐   hamburger ☐
shower ☐   toast ☐   train ☐

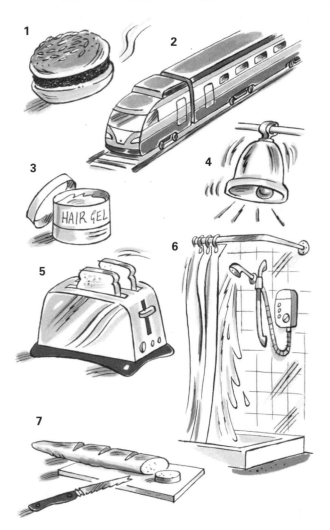

3 Reading

Read the texts on page 40 again. Then read the sentences and write *T* (true) or *F* (false). Correct the false sentences.

1 Will and Rebecca are both 15. ☐
....
2 Rebecca lives in a flat near the sea. ☐
....
3 Will has breakfast at school. ☐
....
4 Will has four lessons before break. ☐
....
5 Rebecca likes music and art. ☐
....
6 Rebecca is at school for seven hours a day. ☐
....
7 Will has eight lessons on Wednesdays. ☐
....
8 Rebecca sometimes has hamburgers for lunch. ☐
....

4 Writing

Write a paragraph about Lucy using this information.

Name: Lucy
Lives in: Melbourne, Australia
Age: 16
Family: two sisters – Ruth (12) and Anne (14)
Weekdays: gets up 7.15am; has a shower/has breakfast 7.45am; leaves home 8.15am; school starts 8.30am; school ends 4pm; plays basketball after school
Favourite lessons: art and English
Weekends: sees family and friends, goes to the cinema, does homework

Lucy lives in Melbourne, Australia.

SIGHTSEEING

1 How many ghosts are there?

1 Reading

Read the text and look at the picture. Find and correct the seven mistakes in the text.

This is a picture of my home town, Westfield. There's a café on the right. There are three tables outside the café. There are five people at the tables and there's a cat. There are two cars in the street. There are two women in the big car. There's a train with lots of people on it. There's a cinema on the left. There are two bicycles outside the café.

1 *There isn't a café on the right. There's a café on the left.*
2
3
4
5
6
7

2 there is/are

Complete the questions about the picture in exercise 1. Then answer them.

1	*Is there a*	street?	*Yes, there is.*
2	*Are there any*	bicycles?	*No, there aren't.*
3		bus?	
4		cars?	
5		café?	
6		shops?	
7		restaurant?	
8		people?	
9		children?	
10		dog?	

3 there is/are

Look at the painting and write a description of the room in your notebook. Use these words and phrases to help you.

> bed   chair   door   pictures   table   window
> on the left/right   on the walls   between   next to

4 How many ... are there?

Write questions and then answer them.

1 minutes/in an hour
How many minutes are there in an hour?
There are sixty minutes in an hour.

2 hands/on a clock

3 days/in a year

4 years/in a century

5 numbers/on a mobile phone

6 players/in a football team

5 one/ones

Write questions and answers.

1 There's a French restaurant./Italian ✗
Is there an Italian one? No, there isn't.

2 There are cinemas./open-air ✓
Are there any open-air ones?

3 There's an old computer./new ✓

4 There's a black bag./blue ✗

5 There are small tables./big ✗

6 There are expensive televisions./cheap ✓

6 Crossword

Complete the crossword.

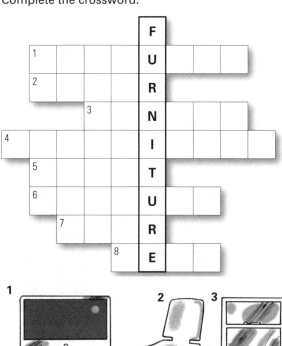

7 Pronunciation

Complete the chart with these words.

> ~~attraction~~   ~~teenager~~   fantastic   cinema   restaurant
> everything   including   museum   gallery   exciting

■ ▪ ▪	▪ ■ ▪
teenager	attraction

Extension   Write a paragraph describing a place in your town in your notebook.

4 SIGHTSEEING

2 She's wearing a long grey coat

1 Reading

Look at the picture and read the text.
Write the people's names.

> This is a picture of our party. Some students are in a band. They're playing some fantastic music. Some students are watching the band and some are dancing. Peter and Julia are dancing. Ian and Sally are watching the band. Stuart is making a phone call and Mindy is taking photos. John is playing the drums. Glynn and Simon are playing the guitar. Next to them is Laura. She's playing the saxophone. At the front is Fiona. She's singing. Everyone is having a good time.

1 *John*
2 _____ and _____
3 _____
4 _____
5 _____ and _____
6 _____ and _____
7 _____
8 _____

2 Spelling

Write the *-ing* form of these verbs.

Verb	-ing form	Verb	-ing form
come	*coming*	open	
cook		practise	
do		read	
draw		run	
get		send	
go		smile	
have		speak	
leave		stop	
make		swim	

3 Present continuous: affirmative

Complete with the present continuous form of these verbs.

> come   listen   look   rain   hold   stand   talk   wear

1 The students *are listening* to a ghost story.
2 The guide _____ about the Grey Lady.
3 We _____ outside the theatre.
4 It's dark and it _____.
5 An actor _____ out of the theatre.
6 I _____ at the actor.
7 She _____ a grey coat.
8 She _____ a red book.

44

4 Present continuous: affirmative

Look at the pictures and find eight differences. Write sentences to compare the pictures using these verbs.

| eat | hold | read | stand | wear |

Picture A
1 *The girl is wearing a skirt.*
2
3
4
5
6
7
8

Picture B
1 *The girl is wearing shorts.*
2
3
4
5
6
7
8

5 Vocabulary

Find six words for clothes and six words for colours in the word square.

T	C	R	H	J	E	A	N	S
C	L	E	S	A	K	V	I	H
P	M	D	D	C	P	D	G	I
B	L	A	C	K	U	N	R	R
L	T	F	O	E	R	Z	E	T
U	C	O	A	T	P	R	Y	L
E	S	J	I	F	L	C	A	P
V	W	H	I	T	E	U	X	N
P	T	R	O	U	S	E	R	S

Now write the words under the correct heading.

Clothes
jeans

Colours

6 Spelling

The same letter is missing in each line. Write the complete words.

1 acto   gey   theate
    actor

2 eatin   holdin   learnin

3 frend   raning   lnes

4 realy   sily   wak

5 wman   famus   utside

6 gost   mont   wite

7 Pronunciation

Do they rhyme (✓) or not? (✗)

1 come   home ☐
2 where   wear ☐
3 grey   way ☐
4 stand   hand ☐
5 comb   home ☐
6 wait   late ☐

Extension Write a description of what you are wearing, holding and carrying at the moment in your notebook. Say what colour these things are.

4 SIGHTSEEING

3 What's she doing?

1 Reading

The group are at the Sea Life Centre in Brighton. Read the dialogue. Then read the sentences and write *T* (true) or *F* (false).

ADAM   This is fantastic. Look at those lovely blue and yellow fish.
EMILY   This is exciting. The fish are swimming over our heads! Where's Teresa?
TERESA   I'm here with Katya. We're taking some photos of the fish.
EMILY   Where's Jake?
ADAM   He's standing next to the shark pool. He's talking to that man over there.
JAKE   Come and watch this!
ADAM   What's happening?
TERESA   Oh, wow! The man is putting his hand in the water. The sharks are coming near him. Oh, now he's opening his hand. He's giving the sharks some food. He's feeding them.
KATYA   Wow! Look at their teeth! Are the sharks biting him?
ADAM   No, they aren't biting him. They're taking the food.
TERESA   Look, now the man is getting into the pool. He's swimming with the sharks!
PIERRE   That's scary!

1 Adam is looking at some blue and yellow fish. ☐
2 Adam and Emily are taking photos. ☐
3 Jake is standing next to the others. ☐
4 Jake is talking to a man. ☐
5 The man is putting his foot into the water. ☐
6 The man is giving the sharks a drink. ☐
7 The sharks are biting the man. ☐
8 Pierre is swimming with the sharks. ☐

2 Present continuous: affirmative and negative

Correct the false sentences from exercise 1.

1 *Adam and Emily aren't taking photos. Katya and Teresa are taking photos.*
2
3
4
5
6

3 Present continuous: questions

Write questions with *What* or *Where* for these answers.

1 *Where's she going?*
   She's going home.
2
   He's wearing a red sweatshirt and black jeans.
3
   They're eating fish and chips.
4
   He's standing next to the shark pool.
5
   They're staying in Brighton.
6
   She's drawing a picture of a shark.
7
   We're sitting on the beach.
8
   They're watching a music programme.

4 Present continuous: questions, short answers and affirmative

Write questions and answers.

1 Diana/cook a meal (make a sandwich)
   Is Diana cooking a meal?
   No, she isn't. She's making a sandwich.

2 Pierre and Adam/run (swim)

3 Ruby/have lunch (eat an ice cream)

4 the people/sing (dance)

5 the actor/tell a joke (learn her lines)

6 you/sleep (study English!)

5 Crossword

Complete the crossword with words for part of the body.

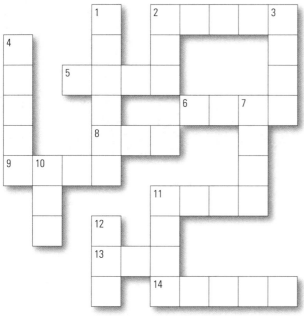

Across →
2 They're white and you use them to eat. (5)
5 It's halfway down your leg. (4)
6 You write with your left or right … (4)
8 You hear with it. (3)
9 You use a comb for it. (4)
11 Your nose is in the centre of it. (4)
13 You see with it. (3)
14 You have one on each hand. (5)

Down ↓
1 You point with it. (6)
2 You have five …s on each foot. (3)
3 You use it when you think. (4)
4 You open it when you speak. (5)
7 You smell with it. (4)
10 Your hand is at the end of it. (3)
11 Plural of *foot*. (4)
12 Your foot is at the end of it. (3)

6 Pronunciation

Find the rhyming words in the box.

| bed | buy | come | goes | ~~here~~ |
| key | know | south | place | there |

1 ear   *here*
2 eye
3 hair
4 head
5 knee
6 mouth
7 nose
8 thumb
9 toe
10 face

7 Pronunciation

Complete the chart with these words.

~~choose~~ ~~cook~~ food good group look pull soup

/ʊ/ **foot**	/uː/ **tooth**
cook	choose

Extension Choose one photo from page 54 of the Student's Book. Write five sentences about what the people are doing in your notebook.

4 SIGHTSEEING

Integrated Skills
Describing places and activities

1 Reading

Look at the painting by Lucy Rawlinson. Then complete the text with these words and phrases.

bed   centre   chest   door
guitar   houses   left   man
picture   right   shirt   shoes
trousers   wall   window

This is a painting of a bedroom. A (**1**) .... is sleeping on the bed in the (**2**) .... of the room. He's wearing a white (**3**) .... and blue (**4**) .... He isn't wearing any (**5**) ....

On the (**6**) .... of the picture, there's an open (**7**) .... It's daytime and you can see two (**8**) .... outside. There's a (**9**) .... by the window. There's a (**10**) .... in the wall at the back of the room. On the (**11**) .... of the picture, there's a small (**12**) .... of drawers next to the (**13**) .... , and there's a (**14**) .... of an animal on the (**15**) ....

2 Writing

Write a description of this painting by Edward Hopper. Use these phrases and the description in exercise 1 to help you.

girl in a café   at a small table   on the right
green coat and a yellow hat   cup of coffee
door on the left   big window behind her
dark outside

48

3 Crossword

Complete the crossword.

Across →

1. Places where you can have meals. (11)
7. The theatre has a famous ... called the Grey Lady. (5)
8. Opposite of *before*. (5)
9. Do you want ... visit the Sea Life Centre? (2)
10. When this happens, you get wet. (4)
12. You smell things with it. (4)
14. The actor is ... a red book. (7)
18. How often do you ... the night at a friend's house? (4)
19. You keep your money in this. (6)

Down ↓

1. Opposite of *left*. (5)
2. A place that sells things. (4)
3. A person who works in a theatre. (5)
4. I'm ... a book about Tutankhamun. (7)
5. You can write new words in your vocabulary ...book. (4)
6. ... . I don't understand. (5)
11. 'Are you singing?' – '..., I'm not.' (2)
13. Opposite of *buy*. (4)
14. Look at that man – ... face is really white! (3)
15. One of seven in a week. (3)
16. Opposite of *old*. (3)
17. You can ... on a chair. (3)

UNIT 4

LEARNER INDEPENDENCE

Classroom English

Match questions 1–5 with answers a–e.

1. What does *enjoy* mean?
2. What's the plural of *woman*?
3. How do you say ![comb] ?
4. Which exercise are we doing?
5. What's the problem?

a. *Women*.
b. I don't understand.
c. The *Classroom English* one.
d. It means *like*.
e. /kəʊm/ – the *b* is silent.

Extensive reading

Read *The Lost Ship* and write the last page of the Captain's log book.

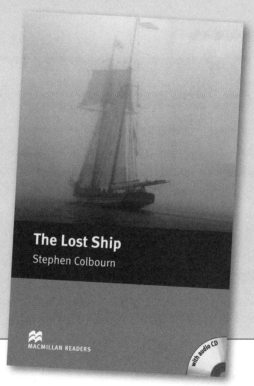

The Captain and his men are looking at the strange ship.
'Hello. Is there anybody there? Can you hear me?'
But there is no answer.

49

4 SIGHTSEEING
Inspiration EXTRA!

REVISION

LESSON 1

Complete the questions with *Is/Are there*. Then answer them for your town.

1 .... lots of shops in your town?
2 .... a museum?
3 .... a beach?
4 How many cinemas .... ?
5 .... an aquarium?
6 .... lots of tourists?

LESSON 2

Complete with the present continuous form of these verbs.

| eat | rain | stand | take | look | ~~visit~~ |

1 The students *are visiting* places in Brighton.
2 Adam .... pictures with his digital camera.
3 Katya and Teresa .... outside the theatre.
4 Adam is going home because it ....
5 Piorro and Jako .... at a map.
6 Emily .... an ice cream.

LESSON 3

Look at this photo and the others on page 54 of the Student's Book. Write questions and short answers.

1 Photo A   the man/sell/hamburgers
   Is the man selling hamburgers? No, he isn't.
2 Photo A   the people/buy/fish and chips

3 Photo B   the girl/ride/a bicycle

4 Photo B   the girl/wear/a helmet

5 Photo C   the people/do/exercises

6 Photo C   the people/stand/on the beach

LESSON 4

Look again at pictures A and B on page 57 of the Student's Book. Write a list of the things you can see in each room.

Picture A
two beds, a desk

Picture B
a wardrobe, some posters

Spelling

Complete these words with silent letters.

1 dau*g*hter 2 ei....ht 3 g....ost 4 ha....f 5 ....nee
6 com.... 7 ....now 8 li....ht 9 lis....en 10 ri....ht
11 s....ience 12 si....ht 13 thum.... 14 toni....ht
15 wa....k 16 wei....ht

Brainteaser

What has four legs, but no head?

Answer on page 53.

UNIT 4

EXTENSION

LESSON 1

Answer the questions about your town. Use the text about Brighton on page 50 of the Student's Book to help you.

My town

1 Where is it?

2 What attractions are there?

3 Are there any ghosts?

4 Is there a place that everyone visits?

LESSON 2

Look at the picture and write a description using these verbs.

hold   pull   rain   sit   smile   wear

LESSON 3

Correct these sentences.

1 Where you are going?

2 Are you haveing lunch?

3 I'm not eat anything.

4 What she talking about?

5 The people isn't listening.

LESSON 4

Write a description of your living room at home.

Web watch

Search for 'Brighton Sea Life Centre' on the Internet and find out more about this fantastic place.

Spelling

These words all end in the sound /ə/ in British English:
broth**er**   doct**or**   met**re**

Complete these words with -er, -or or -re.

1 act *or*   2 calculat......   3 cent......   4 comput......
5 kilomet......   6 numb......   7 pap......   8 photograph......
9 play......   10 sing......   11 teach......   12 teenag......
13 theat......   14 visit......

Brainteaser

What has teeth, but no mouth?

Answer on page 53.

REVIEW
Units 3–4

1 Read and complete. For each number 1–10, choose word or phrase A, B or C.

Dublin is the capital of the Republic of Ireland. Tourists __1__ from all over the world to visit this beautiful city. It's over a thousand years old and is full of history.

__2__ 13th century buildings and the National Museum has fantastic exhibitions. The River Liffey __3__ through the centre of the city and __4__ lots of bridges over the river. How __5__ bridges are there? Go on a river boat and find out! And visit Dublin Zoo in Phoenix Park, which is twice the size of Central Park in New York. But take an umbrella – it __6__ rains in Dublin.

__7__ the evening, you can go on a ghost bus tour and look for Dublin's ghosts. The tour starts __8__ 8pm on weekdays, and at 7pm and 9.30pm __9__ Saturday and Sunday. Or why not see a film? The Irish Film Centre has three cinemas and it __10__ old and new movies. You can also hear fantastic music in Dublin. Half the population is under 25, so it's a great place for young people!

1	**A** are coming	**B** come	**C** comes
2	**A** There's	**B** There are	**C** There has
3	**A** go	**B** goes	**C** going
4	**A** there is	**B** there are	**C** it have
5	**A** lots	**B** any	**C** many
6	**A** often	**B** every	**C** never
7	**A** At	**B** In	**C** On
8	**A** at	**B** in	**C** on
9	**A** at	**B** in	**C** on
10	**A** show	**B** shows	**C** are showing

2 Read the definitions and complete the words.

1	You sit at this to write or work.	d_____
2	You sit at this for meals.	t_____
3	You sit on this.	c_____
4	You sleep on this.	b_____
5	You put clothes in this.	w_____
6	You can look out of this.	w_____
7	You open this to go into a room.	d_____
8	You switch this on when it's dark.	l_____

52

3 Complete the dialogues. Choose A, B or C.

1. Do you like fish?
   - A Yes, I like.
   - B I love it.
   - C That's OK.

2. What does she look like?
   - A She's quite angry.
   - B She has dark hair and brown eyes.
   - C She likes techno and hip-hop.

3. What do you do on Saturday?
   - A Every weekend.
   - B Sorry, I'm busy.
   - C I go to the cinema.

4. Is there a museum in the town?
   - A I'm not sure.
   - B Yes, there are.
   - C Yes, it is.

5. How many chairs are there?
   - A Yes, they are four.
   - B Four ones.
   - C There are four.

4 Find the odd word.

1. carrot (comb) mushroom tomato
2. breakfast lunch dinner weekend
3. afternoon evening minute morning
4. football history maths science
5. aquarium museum theatre tourist
6. eye toe mouth nose
7. bad great lovely nice
8. chair desk flower wardrobe

Answers to Brainteasers

UNIT 3
Revision In the dictionary.
Extension Banana.

UNIT 4
Revision A chair or table.
Extension A comb.

LEARNER INDEPENDENCE
SELF ASSESSMENT

Vocabulary

1 Draw this chart in your notebook. How many words can you write in each category?

More than 10? Good!   *More than 12?* Very good!
More than 15? Excellent!

Food	
Sport and leisure activities	
School subjects	
Parts of the body	
Furniture and equipment	

2 Put the words in order to make expressions from the phrasebooks in Lesson 4 in Units 3 and 4.

1. about what you
   What about you?

2. often how you do here come

3. great sounds that

4. isn't no time there

5. silly oh is this

6. home going I'm

Check your answers.
   6/6 Excellent!   *4/6* Very good!   *2/6* Try again!

My learning diary
In Units 3 and 4:
My favourite topic is

My favourite picture is

The three lessons I like most are

My favourite activity or exercise is

Something I don't understand is

Something I want to learn more about is

5 PEOPLE AND PLACES

1 I'm having a wonderful time

1 Reading

Mr Ward does the same things at the same time every Saturday. Look at his diary and read the text. Find and correct the four mistakes in the text.

Every Saturday, Mr Ward gets up at 7am. At 7.20, he goes swimming at the pool. Then he goes home and he has breakfast at 8.30am. At 10.15, he goes shopping in Brighton. He usually buys food and sometimes he buys clothes and books. He meets his friends, Jim and Sandra, in a café at 10.45 and they have lunch together. In the afternoon, he plays tennis at 2.30. He always plays with Jim, but he never wins. He goes home and watches the news on TV at 6pm. Then at 7.30 he has dinner in a restaurant.

SATURDAY

7am	get up
7.20am	go swimming at the beach
8.30am	have breakfast
10.15am	go shopping
11.45am	meet friends in a café
2.30pm	play tennis with Bob
6pm	watch the news on TV
7.30pm	cook dinner

1   At 7.20, he goes swimming at the beach.
2
3
4

2 Present simple

Look at Mr Ward's diary again and write questions and answers.

1   What time does he get up?
    He gets up at 7am.
2   _____ go swimming?
3
4
5
6
7
8

3 Present continuous

Now it's Saturday. Write sentences about what Mr Ward is doing at these times.

1   am   He's shopping.
2   pm
3   am
4   pm
5   am
6   am
7   am
8   pm

54

UNIT 5

4 Present simple and present continuous

Choose the correct words to complete the sentences.

1	Mr Ward can't answer his mobile because he ….	**A** drives	**B** 's driving (circled)
2	Steven Campbell often … to South-east Asia.	**A** flies	**B** is flying
3	Cathy … to the news on the radio every evening.	**A** listens	**B** is listening
4	Look at Adam! He … with Emily.	**A** plays tennis	**B** 's playing tennis
5	Pierre and Ruby are in the kitchen. They … dinner.	**A** cook	**B** 're cooking
6	We … our friends every evening.	**A** phone	**B** 're phoning
7	Emily is a musician. She … the guitar, the piano and the saxophone.	**A** plays	**B** 's playing
8	That's a long email! Who … to?	**A** do you write	**B** are you writing
9	Jake … to bed late.	**A** often goes	**B** is often going
10	Pierre and Katya … octopus.	**A** don't like	**B** aren't liking

5 Crossword

Look at the pictures on the right. Complete the crossword with the words for jobs and find the missing word ↓.

6 Vocabulary

Match the words in list A with the words and phrases in list B.

	A	B
1	cook	after someone
2	drive	an email
3	listen	history
4	look	a meal
5	play	to the radio
6	teach	a taxi
7	write	the trumpet

(cook is matched to a meal)

7 Pronunciation

Find the rhyming words in the box.

code   ghost   has   one   plane   ~~shirt~~   three   write

1	hurt	*shirt*	5	road	____
2	jazz	____	6	see	____
3	night	____	7	sun	____
4	rain	____	8	most	____

Extension Write about what you do every Saturday in your notebook. Use the text in exercise 1 to help you.

55

5.2 PEOPLE AND PLACES
Whose turn is it?

1 Reading

Read the dialogue. Then match the students with the things.

MR WARD Don't leave your things on the bus! Whose cap is this?
EMILY It's mine. Sorry, Mr Ward.
MR WARD And what about these sunglasses? Are they yours, Teresa?
TERESA No, they aren't mine. I think they're Jake's.
JAKE Yes, they're mine. Sorry, Mr Ward.
ADAM That bag is mine.
PIERRE No, it isn't. It's mine. Your bag is black.
ADAM Oh, yes. Sorry.
MR WARD And here's a watch. Whose watch is this?
ADAM I think it's Katya's. Katya, is it yours?
KATYA No, it isn't, but that's my magazine.
MR WARD Well, whose watch is it?
EMILY Er, Mr Ward. I think it's yours!
MR WARD Oh, yes. Of course. Thank you, Emily. Now please take your things with you!

Emily   Pierre   ~~Katya~~   Mr Ward   Adam   Jake

1   Katya

2 _____

3 _____

4 _____

5 _____

6 _____

2 Whose ...? and possessive 's

Write questions about the things in exercise 1. Then answer them.

1 magazine
  Whose magazine is this? It's Katya's.

2 sunglasses
  _____

3 cap
  _____

4 white bag
  _____

5 watch
  _____

6 black bag
  _____

3 Whose or Who's

Complete with *Whose* or *Who's*.

1 _____ playing on the games console?
2 _____ turn is it now?
3 _____ are those jeans?
4 _____ the boy in the grey sweatshirt?
5 _____ holding the chips?
6 _____ is the blue bag?
7 _____ watch is this?
8 _____ wearing a red cap?

4 Possessive 's or is

Read the sentences. Does 's mean possession or is?

1. It's a great games console. possession ☐ is ✓
2. Emily's playing with Jake. possession ☐ is ☐
3. Is it Teresa's turn? possession ☐ is ☐
4. What's Adam doing? possession ☐ is ☐
5. Jake's T-shirt is black. possession ☐ is ☐
6. Is Teresa's watch silver? possession ☐ is ☐
7. Jake's watching the game. possession ☐ is ☐
8. Adam's phone is ringing. possession ☐ is ☐

5 Possessive pronouns and possessive adjectives

Read the questions and complete the answers.

1. Is that Emily's bag?
   No, it isn't _hers_. _Her_ bag is blue.
2. Is that Jake's T-shirt?
   No, it isn't _____. _____ T-shirt is black.
3. Teresa, are these your keys?
   No, they aren't _____. _____ keys are in my bag.
4. Is this my book, Teresa?
   No, it isn't _____. _____ book is on the desk.
5. Mr Ward, is this our test?
   No, it isn't _____. _____ test is next week.
6. Adam and Ruby, are these your CDs?
   No, they aren't _____. _____ CDs are at home.
7. Is that their car?
   No, it isn't _____. _____ car is red.

6 Punctuation

Rewrite these questions and statements correctly.

1. whose phone is this
   Whose phone is this?
2. i dont know
3. it isnt mine
4. I think its rubys
5. whos ruby
6. shes adams sister

7 Vocabulary

Match the words in list A with the words in list B to make eight compound words. Then write the words.

	A	B		
1	ear	assistant	1	_earring_
2	fire	dresser	2	
3	hair	driver	3	
4	police	fighter	4	
5	shop	glasses	5	
6	sun	officer	6	
7	sweat	ring	7	
8	taxi	shirt	8	

8 Pronunciation

Complete the chart with these words.

~~around~~ ~~bottle~~ camera earring enjoy
guitar console midday police
problem silver sweatshirt

■ ▪	▪ ■
bottle	around

9 Pronunciation

Do they rhyme (✓) or not (✗)?

1. hers — theirs ☐
2. his — quiz ☐
3. their — hair ☐
4. yours — ours ☐
5. good — food ☐
6. turn — learn ☐
7. done — fun ☐
8. whose — those ☐

> **Extension** Rewrite this dialogue correctly in your notebook.
>
> whose bag is this i dont know is it yours emily no it isnt mine my bag is blue i think its katyas katya is it yours yes it is thank you

5.3 PEOPLE AND PLACES
It's sunnier

1 Reading

Read the dialogue. Then read and complete the sentences.

EMILY Oh dear. It's raining again!
TERESA Is it often rainy in Brighton?
EMILY Yes, it is! What's the weather like in Valencia?
TERESA It's always sunny in the summer. Sometimes it rains in the autumn, but not very often. Valencia is very dry – drier than Brighton!
EMILY And I'm sure it's hotter than Brighton.
TERESA Yes, it is. It gets very hot in summer. The sea is much warmer than in Brighton, too.
EMILY Does it get cold in winter?
TERESA No, it's never really cold in Valencia, even in winter!
EMILY You're lucky! Brighton is cold and wet in winter.

1 In summer, _Valencia_ is hotter than _Brighton_.
2 _____ is sunnier than _____.
3 In winter, Brighton is _____ than Valencia.
4 The sea is _____ in Valencia than it is in Brighton.
5 It doesn't often _____ in Valencia, so it is _____ than Brighton.
6 It often _____ in Brighton, so it is _____ than Valencia.

2 Comparative adjectives

Complete the chart.

Adjective	Comparative
angry	angrier
bad	
beautiful	
big	
boring	
dry	
early	
good	
high	
hot	
late	
lucky	
new	
nice	
foggy	
small	

3 Comparative adjectives

Complete with the comparative form of these adjectives.

early   easy   long   ~~old~~   short   sunny

1 Mr Ward is _older_ than Pierre.
2 A kilometre is _____ than 900 metres.
3 Adam's hair is _____ than Katya's hair.
4 Half past six is _____ than twenty to seven.
5 Valencia is _____ than Moscow.
6 English is _____ than Japanese.

58

4 Comparative adjectives

Read the information. Then write sentences using the comparative form of the adjectives in **bold**.

1. Belgium: 30,513 square km **big**
   Switzerland: 41,288 square km
   Switzerland is bigger than Belgium.

2. Spain: 504,748 square km **small**
   Russia: 17,075,400 square km

3. Athens: 25° **hot**
   London: 18°

4. Geneva: 5° **cold**
   Warsaw: 2°

5. Paris: 585mm rain a year **wet**
   Rome: 740mm rain a year

6. Los Angeles: 310mm rain a year **dry**
   New York: 1,200mm rain a year

5 Comparative adjectives

Write your opinion of these things using the comparative form of the adjectives in **bold**.

1. spring/autumn **nice**
   Spring is nicer than autumn.
   OR *Autumn is nicer than spring.*

2. Orlando Bloom/Robert Pattinson **famous**

3. winter/summer **good**

4. science/geography **difficult**

5. football/volleyball **popular**

6. sandwiches/chips **expensive**

6 Vocabulary

Look at the pictures and put the letters in the right order.

1. dwyin — *windy*
2. nirya
3. unysn
4. dluyco
5. nowsy
6. gofgy

7 Vocabulary

Write the opposites.

1. better — *worse*
2. cold
3. difficult
4. earlier
5. good
6. shorter
7. true
8. wet
9. newer
10. wrong

8 Pronunciation

Circle the two rhyming words in each line.

1. (nice)   eyes   (ice)
2. bigger   drier   higher
3. later   waiter   water
4. after   daughter   shorter
5. here   there   year
6. sunny   money   only
7. break   speak   week
8. horse   nurse   worse

> **Extension** What's the weather like in your town in spring, summer, autumn and winter? Write a paragraph in your notebook.

5.4 PEOPLE AND PLACES
Integrated Skills Questionnaire

1 Reading

Read and complete with these words.

> afternoon   clothes   day   favourite   fun   grey
> personality   question   Saturday   weekend

★★★ PERSONALITY TESTS ★★★

Personality tests can tell you what you are like and how you are feeling today, but they can also get things wrong.

Take favourite colours, for example. People say that red or yellow means that you are a confident person, brown or (1) _____ means that you are shy, and blue or green means that you are friendly. But Halle Berry's (2) _____ colours are brown, blue and orange – which means that she is confident, shy and friendly! Beyoncé's favourites are pink, silver and gold – what does that tell us about her (3) _____?

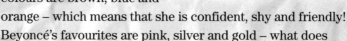

Another popular (4) _____ in personality tests is about your favourite time of the (5) _____. But which day? From Monday to Friday, my favourite time is the (6) _____, when school is over, but on (7) _____ my favourite time is the evening, when I see my friends. People say that liking the afternoon means that you are friendly!

How often do I wear the same (8) _____ the next day? When I go to school, the answer is 'every day' because we have a school uniform. But at the (9) _____ I never wear the same clothes. So is my school personality different from my weekend personality? No, personality tests are (10) _____, but do them quickly and don't be serious about them!

2 Writing

Complete these sentences for you.

1 I'm happy when _____
2 I'm shy when _____
3 I'm careful when _____
4 I'm quiet when _____

3 Crossword

Complete the crossword.

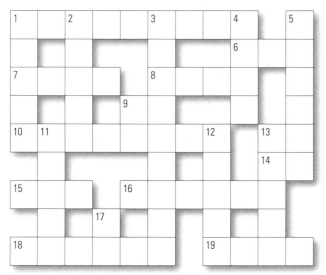

Across →

1. A ... person isn't shy or scared of things. (9)
6. Part of the body – it sounds like *I*. (3)
7. This is our computer. It isn't yours – it's ... (4)
8. You put a ... stop at the end of a sentence. (4)
9. Emily's cousin is in the middle ... the Atlantic Ocean. (2)
10. She's ... English on the phone to her friend in London. (8)
13. Plural of *I*. (2)
14. What's the weather like – is it hot ... cold? (2)
15. Jake's father drives a police ... (3)
16. The season after spring. (6)
18. *now* = at the ... (6)
19. Emily ... her friends at the weekend. (4)

Down ↓

1. Quite angry. (5)
2. This person works in a hospital. (5)
3. Opposite of *easy*. (9)
4. Funny people often ... jokes. (4)
5. Comparative form of *good*. (6)
9. All right. (2)
11. Musical instrument with black and white keys. (5)
12. Football and tennis are ... (5)
13. Comparative form of *bad*. (5)
17. We can't ... sure about the weather. (2)

UNIT 5

LEARNER INDEPENDENCE

Classroom English

Rewrite this dialogue correctly.

EMILY well done teresa
(1) *Well done, Teresa!*

TERESA thanks who wants to play next
(2) _____

ADAM whose turn is it
(3) _____

JAKE i think its mine
(4) _____

EMILY no it isnt yours its adams turn
(5) _____

JAKE sorry but it isnt his it really is mine
(6) _____

ADAM hey whats the problem
(7) _____

Now check your answers on page 66 of the Student's Book.

Extensive reading

Read *The Truth Machine*. Does the truth help anyone in the story?

The Truth Machine is Professor Verity's new invention.
'I love truth,' he says.
Soon everyone wants to use the Truth Machine.
But does the truth help anyone?

5 PEOPLE AND PLACES

Inspiration EXTRA!

REVISION

LESSON 1

Complete with the present simple or present continuous form of the verbs.

1 Teresa's father _plays_ (play) jazz every Saturday night.
2 Emily's mother isn't at home now – she _____ (work) at the hospital.
3 Pierre's mother _____ (teach) French at the moment.
4 We _____ (have) French lessons three times a week.
5 I can't answer the phone – I _____ (wash) my hair.
6 Where _____ you _____ (go)? Can I come with you?
7 Adam's father _____ (fly) planes to South-east Asia.
8 The NFI students _____ (have) a great time in Brighton.

LESSON 2

Rewrite these sentences using possessive adjectives and possessive pronouns.

1 That cap is Emily's.
   It's her cap. It's hers.
2 I have a camera.
3 That computer is Adam and Ruby's.
4 We have lots of magazines.
5 That is Jake's mobile phone.
6 This sandwich is for you.
7 I have a bottle of water.
8 This watch is Teresa's.

LESSON 3

Complete with comparative adjectives.

1 Belgium is _smaller_ (small) than Switzerland.
2 Russia is _____ (big) than Spain.
3 London is _____ (cold) than Athens.
4 Geneva is _____ (hot) than Warsaw.
5 Paris is _____ (dry) than Rome.
6 New York is _____ (wet) than Los Angeles.
7 Valencia is _____ (sunny) than Brighton.
8 Brighton is _____ (foggy) than Valencia.

LESSON 4

Match expressions 1–5 with their meanings. Choose from a–h.

1 It's a beautiful day. [f]
2 Whose turn is it? [ ]
3 What's the problem? [ ]
4 Good idea. [ ]
5 Well done! [ ]

a We're having fun.
b Congratulations!
c What's wrong?
d Don't worry.
e Who goes next?
f The sun is shining.
g It depends.
h I agree.

Spelling

Complete these words from Unit 5.

1 autum___ 2 bre___kfast 3 doct___r 4 firefi___hter
5 fr___endly 6 hi___her 7 jo___rnalist 8 of___en
9 ra___ny 10 temp___rature 11 w___ose

Brainteaser

What goes up, but never comes down?

Answer on page 77.

62

UNIT 5

EXTENSION

LESSON 1

Complete with the present simple or present continuous form of these verbs.

| do | get | have | listen | phone | rain | think |

1 Teresa .... her parents every evening.
2 What .... you .... at the moment?
3 Ssh! I .... to the news on the radio.
4 Jake often .... up late at the weekend.
5 Take your umbrella – I .... it ....
6 .... the students .... a good time in Brighton?

LESSON 2

Look at the picture (also on page 66 of the Student's Book) and read the sentences. What do the words in **bold** mean?

1 Emily is holding **it**.
   Her bag.
2 Jake is holding **them**.
   ....
3 Teresa is wearing silver **ones**.
   ....
4 Adam wears **them** when the sun is shining.
   ....
5 Teresa looks at **it** to check the time.
   ....
6 Emily is wearing **it** on her head.
   ....

LESSON 3

Write sentences comparing these people, places and things.

1 my father/my mother
   My father is taller than my mother.
2 Ruby/Adam
   ....
3 autumn/spring
   ....
4 New York/London
   ....
5 a car/a bicycle
   ....
6 maths/history
   ....

LESSON 4

Write about the personality of two or three family members in your notebook. Use some of these adjectives.

| careful | confident | friendly | happy |
| helpful | open | quiet | serious | shy |

Web watch

Go to www.bbc.co.uk/weather and find out about the weather in different places. What's the weather like in Brighton today?

Spelling

Correct the spelling of these words from Unit 5 by doubling one letter in each word.

1 asi**s**stant   2 beter   3 cros   4 dificult   5 earing
6 hairdreser   7 hapen   8 miday   9 oficer   10 smal
11 sumer   12 suny

Brainteaser

Who is the man in the photo?

I have no brothers or sisters, but this man's mother is my father's daughter.

Answer on page 77.

5 Culture

Social situations

1 Reading and writing

Complete the dialogues with responses a–l.

a Sure.
b ~~See you later.~~
c Bella. What's yours?
d But it's only half past eight!
e I'm looking for my bag.
f Who are you talking about?
g What's wrong?
h Sorry? Can you say that again?
i No, it isn't.
j Yes, I'm sorry. Someone is.
k I live here.
l Nice to meet you.

6 LOOKING BACK

1 Was he the first president?

1 Reading

Adam was very busy last Saturday. Read his diary and answer the questions.

SATURDAY
9.00	meet Emily in the café
10.30	take Ruby to the Sea Life Centre
12.00	lunch at home
2.30	tennis with Pierre at the gym
4.00	meet Teresa, Katya and Jake on the beach
6.00	dinner at Emily's house
8.00	cinema with Emily, Teresa, Katya, Pierre and Jake

1 Where was Adam at 9.30 last Saturday?
   He was in the café.

2 Who was he with at the Sea Life Centre?

3 Where was Adam at 3.00?

4 Where were Katya and Jake at 4.00?

5 Where was Adam at 6.00?

6 Where were the students at 8.30 in the evening?

2 Past simple of *be*: affirmative and negative

Look at the diary in exercise 1 again and correct these sentences.

1 Adam was in the café with Pierre.
   Adam wasn't in the café with Pierre.
   He was in the café with Emily.

2 Adam was at the Sea Life Centre with his mother.

3 Adam was in a restaurant at 12.00.

4 Adam was with Emily at 2.30.

5 Katya and Jake were at the gym at 4.00.

6 The students were at Emily's house at 8.30.

3 Past simple of *be*: affirmative and negative

Follow the lines to find out where the students were at 2.30pm yesterday. Then write sentences.

1 Adam/café   *Adam wasn't in the café.*
2 Emily/park
3 Teresa/cinema
4 Katya and Jake/supermarket
5 Pierre/café

1 Adam
2 Emily
3 Teresa
4 Katya and Jake
5 Pierre

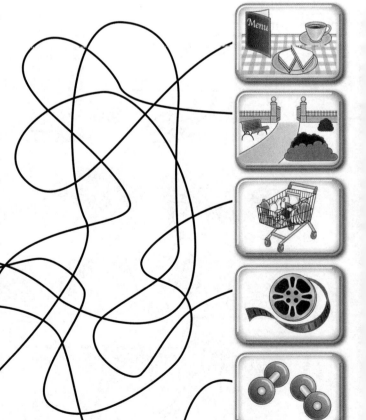

4 Past simple of be: questions and short answers

Write questions and short answers.

This morning at nine o'clock …

1. Mr Ward was on the beach. ✗
   Was Mr Ward on the beach? No, he wasn't.
2. Jake was in the park. ✓
3. Emily was at home. ✗
4. Ruby was at school. ✓
5. Teresa and Katya were in Lewes. ✗
6. Pierre and Adam were in the café. ✓

5 Past simple of be: questions, short answers and affirmative

Where was Steven Campbell last week? Write questions. Then look at the schedule and answer them.

Pilot: Steven Campbell

Monday	London
Tuesday	Tokyo
Wednesday	Tokyo
Thursday	London
Friday	Beijing

1. Monday/Tokyo
   Was Steven in Tokyo on Monday?
   No, he wasn't. He was in London.
2. Tuesday/London
3. Wednesday/Tokyo
4. Thursday/Beijing
5. Friday/London

6 Past simple of be: questions, short answers and affirmative

Write questions and answers.

1. President Kennedy/British (American)
   Was President Kennedy British?
   No, he wasn't. He was American.
2. Salvador Dalí/Italian (Spanish)
3. Marie Curie/Belgian (Polish)
4. Lennon and McCartney/American (British)
5. the Incas/Mexican (Peruvian)
6. the Romans/Spanish (Italian)

7 Vocabulary

Choose the correct words.

1. **in** / on a café
2. on / at the cinema
3. at / in home
4. in / on the beach
5. at / on the gym
6. in / on the park
7. on / at the shopping centre
8. in / on my own

8 Pronunciation

Do they rhyme (✓) or not (✗)?

1	was	cross	☐
2	run	one	☐
3	quite	quiet	☐
4	what	hot	☐
5	moon	town	☐
6	were	there	☐
7	sister	Mr	☐

Extension In your notebook, write a dialogue between you and a friend about last weekend. Where were you both at different times and who were you with?

Me: *Where were you last Saturday at six o'clock? Were you at home?*
James: *No, I was at the cinema.*
Me: *Who were you with?*
James: *I was with my friend, Sam. Where were you last … at …?*

6.2 LOOKING BACK

The Vikings liked music

1 Reading

Do the quiz.

FANTASTIC VIKING FACT QUIZ

1 JORVIK (YORK, IN NORTHERN ENGLAND) WAS FAMOUS AS A PLACE WHERE THE VIKINGS MADE ...
 A chocolate.
 B bread.
 C combs.
 D cars.

2 THE VIKINGS HAD ...
 A bad ships.
 B no houses.
 C good teeth.
 D no money.

3 VIKING MEN OFTEN WORE ...
 A long shirts.
 B long dresses.
 C short skirts.
 D trainers.

4 THE VIKINGS WENT SKATING. THEY MADE SKATES FROM ...
 A wood.
 B horses' feet.
 C silver.
 D knives.

5 IN 850 THE ANGLO-SAXONS ATTACKED A GROUP OF VIKING SHIPS NEAR A PLACE CALLED ...
 A Snack.
 B Hamburger.
 C Lunch.
 D Sandwich.

6 VIKINGS OFTEN ATE WITH THEIR ...
 A hands.
 B arms.
 C feet.
 D toes.

7 VIKING SHIPS SAILED TO ...
 A Mexico.
 B California.
 C Egypt.
 D South America.

8 THE VIKINGS DRANK ...
 A tomato soup.
 B sour cream.
 C tea.
 D beer.

Now check your answers on page 69.

UNIT 6

2 Past simple: affirmative regular verbs

Complete with -d or -ed to make the past simple of these regular verbs.

1 ask*ed* 2 change___ 3 cook___
4 dance___ 5 discuss___ 6 enjoy___
7 hate___ 18 laugh___ 9 look___ 10 love___
11 shout___ 12 smile___ 13 stay___
14 talk___ 15 translate___ 16 watch___

3 Past simple: affirmative regular verbs

Change y to i and add -ed to make the past simple of these regular verbs.

1 carry *carried* 3 cry ___
2 study ___ 4 worry ___

4 Past simple: irregular verbs

Write the past simple of these irregular verbs. Use the list on page 127 of the Student's Book to help you.

Infinitive	Past simple	Infinitive	Past simple
buy	*bought*	say	
do		see	
fly		sing	
get		sit	
give		speak	
hear		steal	
hold		swim	
know		take	
leave		teach	
mean		tell	
meet		think	
read		understand	
run		write	

5 Past simple: affirmative

Read the dialogue on page 46 again. Then complete the sentences with the past simple of these verbs.

ask ~~go~~ be give see take swim get

1 Yesterday, the students ___*went*___ to the Brighton Sea Life Centre.
2 They ___ lots of beautiful fish.
3 Teresa and Katya ___ photos of the fish.
4 Emily ___ Adam where Jake was.
5 Jake ___ next to the shark pool.
6 A man ___ some food to the sharks.
7 Then the man ___ into the pool and ___ with the sharks.

6 Past simple: affirmative

Write true sentences in the past simple using these words and phrases.

Activities

go shopping   go to school   talk to my parents
listen to music   send an email   send a text message
buy a DVD   meet my friends   watch TV

Times

at the weekend   last night   last week
on Monday/Tuesday …   yesterday

1 *I went shopping on Saturday.*
2 ___
3 ___
4 ___
5 ___
6 ___
7 ___

7 Vocabulary

Match the verbs in list A with the words in list B.

	A	B
1	steal	beer
2	be	a board game
3	drink	vegetables
4	eat	money
5	play	jewellery
6	sail	a ship
7	wear	strong

8 Pronunciation

Do they rhyme (✓) or not (✗)?

1	fair	hair	☐
2	steal	feel	☐
3	wore	four	☐
4	clue	two	☐
5	board	word	☐
6	bread	said	☐
7	place	plays	☐
8	beer	hear	☐

Extension Write five sentences in your notebook about what you did last week.

FANTASTIC VIKING FACT QUIZ ANSWERS:
1 c 2 c (no sweets!) 3 a 4 b 5 d 6 a 7 c 8 d

6
3 Did he say sorry?

LOOKING BACK

THE LEGEND OF DEVIL'S DYKE

The students enjoyed their visit to Devil's Dyke. They left the minibus at the top of the hill and walked down into the V-shaped valley. It was about 100 metres from the top of the hill to the bottom of the valley. From the top, they saw the sea and the Isle of Wight. They also found lots of beautiful flowers there. People call the place Devil's Dyke because, many years ago, people thought that the devil made the valley. They said he

didn't like the fact that there were so many churches in the area, so, one night, he dug a deep valley from the sea to the towns. But an old woman heard him and she got out of bed. She lit a candle and put it by her window. The devil saw the light in her cottage and thought it was morning. The devil ran away and didn't finish the valley, so the sea didn't reach the churches.

1 Reading

Read the text. Then read and correct the sentences.

1 The students stayed in the minibus.
   The students didn't stay in the minibus. They left the minibus at the top of the hill.

2 They cycled down into the valley.

3 The devil made the valley in the day.

4 The old woman switched on a light.

5 She put the candle by her door.

6 The devil thought it was evening.

7 The devil swam away.

2 Past simple: questions and short answers

Look at the chart. Then write questions about what the students did yesterday and answer them.

	Pierre	Teresa	Adam and Ruby
go shopping	✗	✓	✗
help in the house	✓	✗	✓
send a text message	✗	✓	✓

1 *Did* Pierre *go shopping?*
   No, he didn't.

2 *Did* Teresa *go shopping?*
   Yes, she did.

3 _____ Adam and Ruby _____

4 _____ Pierre *help in the house?*

5 _____ Teresa _____

6 _____ Adam and Ruby _____

7 _____ Pierre _____

8 _____ Teresa _____

9 _____ Adam and Ruby _____

3 Past simple: questions and short answers

Write questions about yesterday and answer them for you.

1. go to school
   Did you go to school yesterday?
   Yes, I did.   OR   *No, I didn't.*

2. have breakfast

3. go to bed early

4. clean your room

5. borrow something from a friend

6. go to the park

7. wear any jewellery

8. lose anything

4 Past simple: questions, short answers and affirmative

Write questions and answers.

1. Emily/have a piano lesson on Tuesday (Friday)
   Did Emily have a piano lesson on Tuesday?
   No, she didn't. She had a piano lesson on Friday.

2. Katya/write a letter to her sister (parents)

3. Jake/play basketball at the weekend (football)

4. Ruby and Adam/cook a meal on Saturday (Sunday)

5. Teresa/get a text message from Katya (Emily)

6. the students/go cycling in Brighton (swimming)

7. Adam/lose Pierre's MP3 player (camera)

8. Teresa/buy a present for her mother (father)

5 Spelling

The same letter is missing in each line. Write the complete words.

1. apologis   camra   worrid
2. anythin   riht   wron
3. lisen   laer   yeserday
4. agry   roud   runing
5. caried   foget   sory

6 Pronunciation

Complete the chart with these words.

across   agree   explain   evening   forget
listen   mistake   open   visit   window

■□	□■
across	

Extension Read the story on page 81 of the Student's Book. Then invent another ghost story and write it in your notebook.

6.4 LOOKING BACK
Integrated Skills Telling a story

1 Reading and writing
Complete this story about Dracula with *and*, *but* and *then*.

Jo and her brother Chris were on holiday in Transylvania in Romania. One day, when they were out walking, there was a terrible storm. The teenagers were soon very wet (1) _____ they wanted to escape from the wind and rain. They had a map, (2) _____ they didn't know where they were. (3) _____ they saw a huge empty castle – Castle Dracula. The door was open (4) _____ Jo and Chris ran in.

It was dark and cold in the castle. 'Come on,' Jo said. 'Let's explore.' The teenagers walked through the empty rooms, (5) _____ they didn't find anything. (6) _____ Chris stopped and said, 'Look, there's a strange wardrobe!' He went over (7) _____ opened the wardrobe door.

Chris ran back to Jo. 'There's someone in the wardrobe!' he shouted. In the wardrobe, they saw a tall man with shining eyes. 'It's Dracula!' Chris shouted.
'(8) _____ I thought he was dead,' Jo replied.
(9) _____ Dracula started to walk across the room. Chris put his arm round his sister.

Jo opened her jacket. Around her neck, she had some silver jewellery. When Dracula saw the jewellery, he stopped (10) _____ put his hands to his eyes. 'Vampires hate silver and light,' Jo said. 'Quick! Let's run!' Chris replied. (11) _____ something strange happened. Suddenly, Dracula put down his hands (12) _____ started to laugh. 'Don't worry. I'm not a vampire. Were you really scared?' he asked. Jo and Chris looked at each other. 'Yes,' Chris replied. 'OK, you aren't Dracula. Who are you?' 'I'm an actor,' the man replied. 'This is the Transylvanian Dracula Experience – it's very popular with tourists.'

2 Crossword

Complete the crossword.

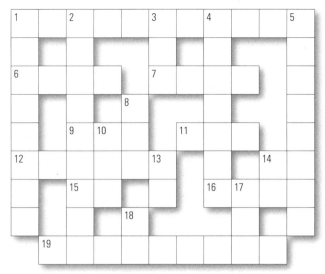

Across →

1. It's very hot – the ... is 32°C. (11)
6. Past simple of *read*. (4)
7. At night it gets ... (4)
9. '... wrote *Dracula*?' 'Bram Stoker.' (3)
11. Infinitive of *ran*. (3)
12. 'I can't see him.' 'He's ... you!' (6)
14. True ... false? (2)
15. What ... the time? (2)
16. Opposite of *there*. (4)
19. Earrings are a kind of ... (9)

Down ↓

1. Very bad. (8)
2. At the same time as something else is happening. (9)
3. The colour of blood. (3)
4. Some Vikings went ... Europe to Asia. (7)
5. Leif Eriksson was a famous Viking ... (8)
8. Past simple of *win*. (3)
10. They found Dracula outside ... castle. (3)
13. Infinitive of *did*. (2)
14. Black ... white coffee? (2)
17. You hear with your ...s. (3)
18. Excuse ... (2)

UNIT 6

LEARNER INDEPENDENCE

Classroom English

Match questions 1–5 with answers a–e.

1. Did you say 'thirteen' or 'thirty'? ☐
2. What page did she say? ☐
3. I'm sorry, what exercise did you say? ☐
4. How long do we have? ☐
5. What's the time? ☐

a. Three minutes.
b. Exercise 3.
c. It's time for break.
d. Page five.
e. Thirty.

Extensive reading

Read *The House in the Picture* and *Abbot Thomas' Treasure*. Which story did you like best? Why?

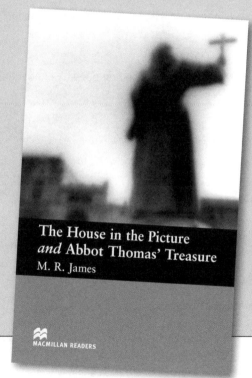

Two nineteenth-century ghost stories:

The House in the Picture
Mr Williams had an old picture of a house. It wasn't a very good picture. It wasn't a very interesting picture. But then the picture told Mr Williams a terrible story.

Abbot Thomas' Treasure
An archaeologist found some gold in an old church. Someone buried the gold 300 years ago. But someone, or something, didn't want the archaeologist to keep the gold.

6 LOOKING BACK
Inspiration EXTRA!

REVISION

LESSON 1

Write questions and short answers.

1 Spain was the winner of the 2010 World Cup. ✓
   Was Spain the winner of the 2010 World Cup?
   Yes, it was.

2 Picasso was from Spain. ✓
   ....

3 Venus Williams was a champion at the age of 17. ✗
   ....

4 The 2008 Olympic Games were in China. ✓
   ....

5 Oprah Winfrey was the first woman to win a Nobel Prize. ✗
   ....

6 Tenzing and Hillary were the first people on the moon. ✗
   ....

7 Pompeii was a Roman volcano. ✗
   ....

8 The Aztecs were from Mexico. ✓
   ....

LESSON 2

Complete with the past simple of these verbs.

| ~~come~~ eat discover like sail find visit wear |

1 The Vikings *came* from Scandinavia.
2 The Vikings .... across the sea in fantastic ships.
3 They .... music and board games.
4 Viking men and women .... jewellery.
5 The Vikings .... lots of fruit and vegetables.
6 Archaeologists .... lots of clues about Viking life in Britain.
7 The Vikings .... lots of countries.
8 Leif Eriksson .... North America before Columbus.

LESSON 3

Read the sentences. Then look at exercise 4 on page 81 of the Student's Book and write questions and short answers.

1 The girl wore a long red dress.
   Did the girl wear a long red dress? No, she didn't.

2 The girl smiled at Pierre.

3 The girl went into a shop.

4 Pierre ran in after her.

5 Pierre closed his eyes.

6 Pierre thought the girl was Teresa.

7 Pierre called Teresa on his mobile.

8 Adam said Teresa was with him.

LESSON 4

Think of a film or book about ghosts or vampires. Write about what happened in your notebook.

Spelling

Complete these words from Unit 6.

1 acro....s 2 at....ack 3 bor....ow 4 dres.... 5 final....y
6 hap....en 7 jewel....ery 8 mat....er 9 shop....ing
10 sor....y 11 ter....ible 12 wor....ied

Brainteaser

We pronounce it like one letter, but it has three letters and everyone has two of them.

Answer on page 77.

UNIT 6

EXTENSION

LESSON 1

Write sentences about where you were and who you were with at different times yesterday. Use these phrases to help you.

> at home   at school   at …'s house   in the park
> at the shopping centre   in a café   at the cinema
> in bed   on a bus   in a car

7am *At 7am, I was at home with my mother and father.*
10am
12pm
4pm
5pm
6pm
7pm
8pm
10pm
12am

LESSON 2

Write about what you did on your last holiday using the past simple of these verbs.

> visit   stay at   wear   go to   have   play   watch   meet

LESSON 3

Look at exercise 7 on page 81 of the Student's Book. Choose three of the activities and write three dialogues in your notebook using the question words *What*, *When* and *Where*.

A: *Did you watch TV last night?*
B: *Yes, I did.*
A: *What did you watch?*
B: *The Simpsons.*
A: *When did you watch it?*
B: *At seven thirty.*
A: *Where did you watch it?*
B: *At my friend's house.*

LESSON 4

Write a diary entry for one day last week in your notebook.

Web watch

Search for 'Devil's Dyke' and 'Brighton' on the Internet and find out more about what you can do and see there.

Spelling

The sound /iː/ is often spelt *ea* or *ee*: Pl*ea*sed to m*ee*t you. Complete these sentences with words containing *ea* or *ee*.

1 When you are hungry, you want to ___eat___.
2 There are seven days in a _____.
3 When you are tired, you want to _____.
4 When you go away from a place, you _____ it.
5 The Vikings sailed to Britain to _____ silver and gold.
6 The Vikings ate _____, fish, fruit and vegetables.
7 Jonathan Harker didn't _____ Dracula in the day.
8 A _____ is someone between the age of 13 and 19.

Brainteaser

What can you find in the middle of both Australia and America?

Answer on page 77.

75

REVIEW
Units 5-6

1 Read and complete. For each number 1–12, choose word or phrase A, B or C.

Grace Darling

It was early morning on 7th September 1838 in the Longstone Lighthouse, in the north of England. Grace Darling, 22 years old, __1__ in the lighthouse with her mother and father.

There __2__ a terrible storm and Grace heard the sound of the wind and the sea. But there was something else. What was it? Grace looked out into the storm. She __3__ a shout from the sea. Then Grace saw where the shout __4__ from. She ran to her parents' room. 'Quick, Father, look – there's a ship! It's on the Big Harcar Rock.'

'Yes, you're right,' her father __5__. 'And there are men on the ship.'

The ship was over a kilometre away from the lighthouse and there __6__ much time.

Father and daughter ran to the lighthouse's rowing boat. They __7__ the small boat into the sea.

'Now you stay here,' William, Grace's father, said.

'No,' replied Grace. 'I'm coming with you. You can't go __8__.'

The sea was very high and it was hard to row to the ship. When they __9__ to Big Harcar Rock, they found nine men. They helped five of the men into their little boat. It wasn't easy and Grace almost __10__ into the water. Then they rowed back to the lighthouse. Grace stayed at the lighthouse with three of the men. William and two of the men __11__ back to the ship for the others.

William and Grace saved the lives of nine men that day. Grace became famous and people __12__ about her in the newspapers. But she didn't leave the lighthouse or her parents. Four years later, she became ill and died, but her name lived on after her death.

1	A lives	B is living	C lived
2	A be	B was	C were
3	A heard	B listened	C saw
4	A came	B come	C comes
5	A reply	B replies	C replied
6	A was	B wasn't	C weren't
7	A put	B puts	C putting
8	A only	B own	C alone
9	A get	B gets	C got
10	A fall	B fell	C feel
11	A go	B going	C went
12	A read	B reading	C reads

2 Read the definitions and complete the words.

1 I help people to learn things. t _____
2 I look after people who are ill or hurt. d _____
3 I fly planes. p _____
4 I write newspaper articles. j _____
5 I work in a restaurant and take food to the tables. w _____
6 When people are speaking, I translate their words into another language. i _____
7 I play the guitar in a band. m _____
8 I work in films and in the theatre. a _____

3 Complete the dialogues. Choose A, B or C.

1 Well done!
   A What did you do?
   B Thank you.
   C That's all right.

2 What's the weather like?
   A No, I don't like it.
   B It's getting late.
   C It's hot and sunny.

3 Excuse me, is this your bag?
   A Yes, it's yours.
   B No, it isn't mine.
   C Good idea!

4 What's the matter?
   A I can't find my wallet.
   B It's a book about pop music.
   C Let's have a party.

5 I'm sorry I'm late.
   A See you later.
   B Don't worry.
   C Of course not.

4 Find the odd word.

1 silver   gold   jewellery   vegetable
2 save   kill   attack   steal
3 huge   tall   bread   strong
4 fly   boat   sail   drive
5 flower   explorer   composer   hairdresser
6 Europe   Ireland   Asia   Africa
7 plane   train   horse   ship
8 fabulous   terrible   wonderful   fantastic

Answers to Brainteasers

UNIT 5
Revision Your age.
Extension The woman's son.

UNIT 6
Revision Eye.
Extension The letter *r*.

LEARNER INDEPENDENCE
SELF ASSESSMENT

Vocabulary

1 Draw this chart in your notebook. How many words can you write in each category?

More than 10? Good!   *More than 12?* Very good!
More than 15? Excellent!

Jobs	
Weather	
Transport	
Town facilities	

2 Put the words in order to make expressions from the phrasebooks in Lesson 4 in Units 5 and 6.

1 time to it's …
   It's time to …

2 turn it whose is

3 matter what's the

4 honest be to …

5 mean do what you

6 it about forget let's

Check your answers.
6/6 Excellent!   *4/6* Very good!   *2/6* Try again!

My learning diary
In Units 5 and 6:

My favourite topic is

My favourite picture is

The three lessons I like most are

My favourite activity or exercise is

Something I don't understand is

Something I want to learn more about is

7 TAKING ACTION

1 What are you going to do?

1 Reading

Read Katya's email to an American friend. Then answer the questions.

From: katya@livemail.com
To: cindy@himail.com
Subject: Lots to do!

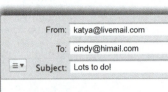

Hi, Cindy!
Oh dear! It's almost the end of the exchange and there are lots of things I want to do!

This afternoon I'm going to buy presents for my family – I'm not going to forget anyone! When I went to Germany last year, I forgot to get something for Dima and he was really angry. I'm going to buy Anna a guide to London because she's going to spend two weeks there in the summer holidays. My mother is going to be in London with Anna. But I can't get her a guide to London because I'm going to get one for Anna! Mmm – I know! Mum is going to learn Italian this autumn. I can get her an Italian textbook and CD.

My father isn't going to visit London this summer because he's very busy at work. He's going to go walking in the mountains with some friends. So I'm going to get him a nice hat for the mountains. Then I'm going to get some English chocolate for my grandparents. I'm not going to have time to do anything else, so I'm not going to write any more emails!

Love,
Katya

1 What is Katya going to do this afternoon?
   She's going to buy presents for her family.

2 What is she going to get for Anna?

3 Who is going to London with Anna?

4 What is Katya's mother going to do this autumn?

5 Why isn't Katya's father going to London?

6 What is Katya going to buy for her grandparents?

2 *going to*: affirmative and negative

Write sentences.

1 the Black Eyed Peas/do a European tour/American tour
   The Black Eyed Peas aren't going to do a European tour. They're going to do an American tour.

2 the Campbells/have a pizza party/barbecue

3 Ruby/play a computer game/board game

4 Pierre/eat octopus for breakfast/eggs

5 Jake/listen to Miley Cyrus/Dizzee Rascal

6 Teresa/go to the cinema/the gym

3 *going to*: questions and short answers

Write questions and short answers.

1 Katya/buy lots of presents ✓
   Is Katya going to buy lots of presents?
   Yes, she is.

2 Jake/stay in Brighton after the exchange ✗

3 Ruby and Adam/have a barbecue ✓

4 the barbecue/be on Sunday ✓

5 all the students/be at the barbecue ✓

6 you/visit Brighton next week ✗

UNIT 7

4 Why ...? Because ...

Write questions about what the students are doing. Then answer them using *going to* and these phrases.

do her homework	go running	go skateboarding
go swimming	go shopping	have a guitar lesson
play tennis	~~see a film~~	

1 Katya/hold a cinema ticket

Why is Katya holding a cinema ticket?
Because she's going to see a film.

2 Jake and Pierre/wear tennis clothes

3 Diana/hold a bag

4 Adam/carry a skateboard

5 Emily/carry a guitar

6 Ruby/hold some books

7 Pierre/wear trainers

8 Teresa and Emily/carry swimming things

5 Vocabulary

Match the verbs in list A with the words and phrases in list B.

	A	B
1	call	worried
2	have	an ambulance
3	speak to	someone's leg
4	look	someone
5	watch	a competition
6	wear	shorts
7	win	an accident
8	X-ray	a DVD

6 Vocabulary

Complete with these words.

| X-ray | ambulance | barbecue | accident | holiday |
| message | programme | prize | worried | DVD |

1 People who are ill can go to hospital in an _____.

2 You look _____. What's the matter?

3 He wasn't at home so I left a _____ with his brother.

4 A _____ is a party where you cook things outside.

5 The winner of a competition usually gets a _____.

6 You can watch films on a _____ player.

7 *The Simpsons* is my favourite TV _____.

8 We're going to fly to Hawaii for a _____ in the summer!

9 He had an _____ in his car, but he's going to be OK.

10 He hurt his arm so the doctors are going to _____ it.

7 Pronunciation

Do they rhyme (✓) or not (✗)?

1	wrong	going	☐
2	know	no	☐
3	buy	why	☐
4	prize	eyes	☐
5	lose	nose	☐
6	wear	dear	☐
7	speak	week	☐
8	want	can't	☐

Extension A friend phoned you. She had an accident and is in hospital. The doctors are going to X-ray her leg. She wants you to go to the hospital to see her. Write a message to your parents in your notebook. Tell them what happened and what you're going to do.

7 TAKING ACTION

2 She loves skateboarding

1 Reading

Read the dialogue. Then read the sentences and write T (true) or F (false).

TERESA   What are you reading, Emily?
EMILY   It's a magazine about the stars. There's an article about what they like doing in their free time.
TERESA   Really?
EMILY   Yes. Did you know that Halle Berry enjoys painting and she gives her pictures to friends at Christmas?
TERESA   No, I didn't know that. Johnny Depp likes painting as well, I think. And I read somewhere that Sylvester Stallone likes it, too.
EMILY   Yes, that's right. Look there are photos of some of their paintings. They're quite good. And it says here that Kylie Minogue likes playing word games.
TERESA   Well, she likes words – she writes her own songs, I think. What about sports stars? They don't get a lot of free time because they practise every day.
EMILY   When she isn't playing in tennis tournaments, Venus Williams loves designing clothes.
TERESA   That's interesting. Does she wear the clothes she designs?
EMILY   I don't know. The article doesn't say and there aren't any photos of her.
TERESA   Are there any funny things in the article?
EMILY   Well, it says that Cameron Díaz likes eating caviar and chips. That's funny.
TERESA   Why is it funny?
EMILY   Caviar is very expensive and chips are cheap.
TERESA   What's caviar?
EMILY   Fish eggs.
TERESA   Oh!

1 Johnny Depp gives Halle Berry paintings for Christmas. ☐
2 Both Halle Berry and Sylvester Stallone enjoy painting. ☐
3 Johnny Depp doesn't like painting. ☐
4 Kylie Minogue doesn't write her own songs. ☐
5 Venus Williams likes designing clothes. ☐
6 The article has photos of Venus Williams wearing the clothes she designs. ☐
7 Cameron Díaz hates eating fish eggs. ☐

2 Verb + gerund

Write sentences.

1 I/like/dance
   I like dancing.

2 she/enjoy/play golf

3 they/love/sail

4 you/enjoy/cook

5 we/like/watch TV

6 he/love/painting and drawing

3 Verb + gerund

Write sentences.

love ☆☆☆   enjoy ☆☆   not mind ☆   not like ★   hate ★★

1 Adam/play chess ☆☆☆
   Adam loves playing chess.

2 Pierre/lose tennis games ★★

3 Emily/listen to Beyoncé ☆☆☆

4 Pierre/iron shirts ★

5 Jake/cook ☆

6 Teresa/go to the cinema ☆☆

UNIT 7

4 Verb + gerund

Write questions and answers.

1 Jake/like/dance (love)

   Does Jake like dancing? Yes, he loves it.

2 Teresa/enjoy/go to museums (hate)

3 Teresa and Emily/hate/sing (like)

4 Pierre/hate/go to the cinema (enjoy)

5 Adam/mind/do his homework (not mind)

6 Ruby and Adam/mind/help their mum (like)

7 Emily/love/run (not like)

8 Katya/like/ride (love)

5 Verb + gerund

Write questions and answer them for you.

1 like/play chess

   Do you like playing chess?
   No, I don't. I hate playing chess.

2 enjoy/cook

3 love/dance

4 like/swim

5 mind/help at home

6 hate/clean your room

6 Crossword

Complete the crossword and find the missing word ↓.

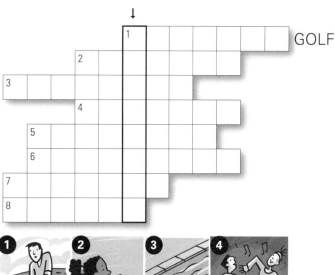

7 Vocabulary

Match the words in list A with the words and phrases in list B.

	A	B
1	play	a scarf
2	jump	a horse
3	knit	out of a plane
4	paint	pictures
5	swim	ice hockey
6	ride	songs
7	write	with sharks

8 Pronunciation

Do they rhyme (✓) or not (✗)?

1 knit   night ☐   5 ride   died   ☐
2 mind   kind   ☐   6 dive   give   ☐
3 hate   wait   ☐   7 like   bike   ☐
4 free   sea   ☐   8 golf   half   ☐

Extension Write five sentences in your notebook saying which activities you love/like/don't like/hate/don't mind doing.

7 TAKING ACTION

3 The most dangerous animal

1 Reading

Read the dialogue. Then look at the pictures and write sentences using the superlative form of *big*, *dangerous*, *fast* or *tall*.

RUBY   Adam and Pierre, can you help me with my homework?
PIERRE   Sure.
ADAM   OK. What's it about?
RUBY   Animals. What's the biggest animal?
ADAM   That's easy. It's the elephant.
PIERRE   I'm not sure. The elephant is the biggest land animal, but I think the whale is the biggest animal.
RUBY   What about the fastest land animal?
ADAM   The cheetah?
PIERRE   Yes, definitely. It's the cheetah. But the falcon is faster, so that's the fastest bird.
RUBY   What's the fastest fish?
PIERRE   I have no idea. Adam?
ADAM   I think it's the sailfish.
RUBY   The next one's easy. The tallest animal is the giraffe and the most dangerous fish is the shark. But what's the most dangerous animal?
ADAM   Mum, when she's angry with us!
RUBY   Don't be silly, Adam.
ADAM   OK then. I think it's the lion or the tiger … or what about the bear?
PIERRE   I think it's something much smaller, like the mosquito because it can give you malaria.
ADAM   That's right. But a mosquito is an insect.
PIERRE   Yes, but it's still an animal.

The elephant is the biggest land animal.

2 Superlative adjectives

Complete the chart.

Adjective	Superlative
slow	*the slowest*
short	
tall	
small	
young	
big	
wet	
strange	
ugly	
amazing	
boring	
exciting	
popular	
good	
bad	

3 Superlative adjectives

Complete the sentences using the superlative form of these adjectives.

cold   dry   ~~high~~   hot   sunny   wet

1 At 8,850 metres, Mount Everest is ___*the highest*___ mountain in the world.
2 With 1cm of rain a year, and no rain at all in some years, the Atacama Desert in Chile is _____ place in the world.
3 With 4,055 hours of sun a year, Yuma in Arizona in the USA is _____ place in the world.
4 With 1,270cm of rain a year, Mawsynram in north-east India is _____ place in the world.
5 At a temperature of –89.4° C, Antarctica is _____ continent in the world.
6 At a temperature of 57.8° C, El Azizia in Libya is _____ place in the world.

4 Spelling

The same letter is missing in each line. Write the complete words.

1 dangrous   frindliest   tomatos   programm

2 amzing   beutiful   disese   malari

3 excting   anmal   millon   fles

4 scard   peopl   levl   countris

5 talest   smalest   footbal   caled

5 Vocabulary

Find 13 words for animals in the word square.

B	O	P	S	C	A	T	L	F
E	L	E	P	H	A	N	T	A
A	S	N	A	E	R	C	I	L
W	H	G	R	E	D	O	G	C
H	A	U	R	T	P	W	E	O
A	R	I	O	A	L	I	R	N
L	K	N	T	H	I	P	P	O
E	F	G	I	R	A	F	F	E

6 Pronunciation

Complete the chart with these words.

~~amazing~~   ~~animal~~   dangerous   elephant   exciting
including   mosquito   octopus   scientist   unhappy

■□□	□■□
animal	*amazing*

Extension In your notebook, write sentences about TV programmes using the superlative form of these adjectives.

amazing   bad   boring   exciting
good   long   popular   short

The shortest programme on TV is the news.

7 TAKING ACTION

4 Integrated Skills Messages

1 Reading

Read the questions and answers. Choose the correct words.

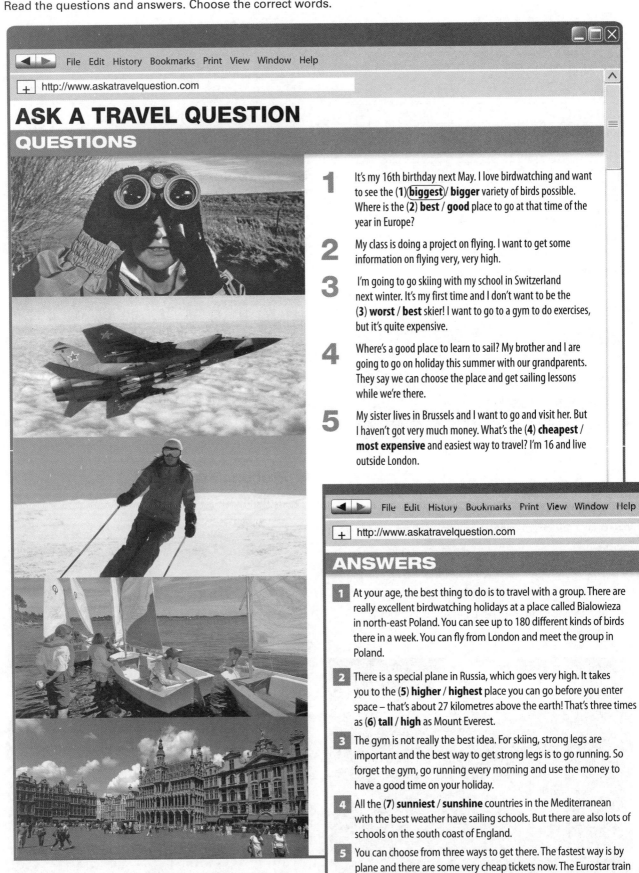

ASK A TRAVEL QUESTION

QUESTIONS

1. It's my 16th birthday next May. I love birdwatching and want to see the (1) **biggest** / **bigger** variety of birds possible. Where is the (2) **best** / **good** place to go at that time of the year in Europe?

2. My class is doing a project on flying. I want to get some information on flying very, very high.

3. I'm going to go skiing with my school in Switzerland next winter. It's my first time and I don't want to be the (3) **worst** / **best** skier! I want to go to a gym to do exercises, but it's quite expensive.

4. Where's a good place to learn to sail? My brother and I are going to go on holiday this summer with our grandparents. They say we can choose the place and get sailing lessons while we're there.

5. My sister lives in Brussels and I want to go and visit her. But I haven't got very much money. What's the (4) **cheapest** / **most expensive** and easiest way to travel? I'm 16 and live outside London.

ANSWERS

1. At your age, the best thing to do is to travel with a group. There are really excellent birdwatching holidays at a place called Bialowieza in north-east Poland. You can see up to 180 different kinds of birds there in a week. You can fly from London and meet the group in Poland.

2. There is a special plane in Russia, which goes very high. It takes you to the (5) **higher** / **highest** place you can go before you enter space – that's about 27 kilometres above the earth! That's three times as (6) **tall** / **high** as Mount Everest.

3. The gym is not really the best idea. For skiing, strong legs are important and the best way to get strong legs is to go running. So forget the gym, go running every morning and use the money to have a good time on your holiday.

4. All the (7) **sunniest** / **sunshine** countries in the Mediterranean with the best weather have sailing schools. But there are also lots of schools on the south coast of England.

5. You can choose from three ways to get there. The fastest way is by plane and there are some very cheap tickets now. The Eurostar train is also fast and can be cheaper than a plane. The cheapest way is by bus and boat, but it's also the (8) **slower** / **slowest**.

2 Writing

Write two questions for the website about your country. Then write the answers.

Questions

1 _____

2 _____

Answers

1 _____

2 _____

3 Crossword

Complete the crossword.

Across →
1. When you win a ..., you get a prize. (11)
5. The biggest land animals. (9)
7. What kind of food do whales ...? (3)
9. It's called a pullover because you ... it over your head. (4)
10. True information. (4)
11. The first two letters of the alphabet. (2)
14. I want to ... on a sailing holiday. (2)
16. The colour of planet Mars. (3)
18. You can find the meaning of words in a ... (10)

Down ↓
1. Opposite of *expensive*. (5)
2. Something or someone that lots of people like is ... (7)
3. There are eleven players in a football ... (4)
4. A mosquito is an ... (6)
6. 'Do you like riding?' 'Yes, I love ...' (2)
8. 'Where's Teresa?' 'She's ... the cinema.' (2)
12. Superlative of *good*. (4)
13. Opposite of *beautiful*. (4)
15. Opposite of *new*. (3)
17. Sports... and sportswomen. (3)

LEARNER INDEPENDENCE

Classroom English

Complete with these words.

again   borrow   suggest   excuse   turn   way

1. Whose _____ is it now?
2. _____ me, what page is it?
3. Can I _____ your book, please?
4. What is the best _____ to do this exercise?
5. Please can you say that _____?
6. What do you _____ I do now?

Extensive reading

Read *Jane Eyre*. Does the story have a happy ending?

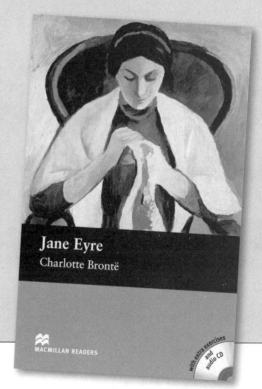

The nineteenth century. The north of England. Jane Eyre has no parents and no money. She goes to work for Mr Rochester at his house, Thornfield Hall. Jane likes Mr Rochester, but soon she is scared of something in the house.

7 TAKING ACTION
Inspiration EXTRA!

REVISION

LESSON 1

Write questions and answers with *going to*.

1 what/Teresa/read (her new magazine)
   What is Teresa going to read?
   She's going to read her new magazine.

2 who/Pierre/phone (Adam)

3 where/Katya/go (the gym)

4 what/Jake/play (tennis)

5 what/Emily/practise (the piano)

LESSON 2

Correct these sentences.

1 Avril Lavigne hates skateboarding.
   Avril Lavigne doesn't hate skateboarding.
   She loves skateboarding.

2 Johnny Depp hates painting.

3 Cameron Díaz hates knitting.

4 Robert Pattinson hates skiing.

5 Johnny Depp loves dancing.

6 Orlando Bloom hates skydiving.

LESSON 3

Write sentences.

1 cheetah/slow animal ✗/fast animal ✓
   The cheetah isn't the slowest animal.
   It's the fastest animal.

2 falcon/dangerous bird ✗/fast bird ✓

3 tiger/boring animal ✗/exciting animal ✓

4 shark/friendly fish ✗/dangerous fish ✓

5 giraffe/big animal ✗/tall animal ✓

6 mosquito/small insect ✗/dangerous insect ✓

LESSON 4

Look at the sketch *Superlative Holidays!* on page 98 of the Student's Book. Then write a short dialogue between a travel agent and a customer in your notebook.

   Customer: Hello. I want to book a holiday.
   Travel agent: What kind of holiday? The …

Spelling

Correct the spelling of these words from Unit 7.

1 barbicue   *barbecue*
2 dangerus
3 finesh
4 melaria
5 compitition
6 diseese
7 medecine
8 sceintist

Brainteaser

Which is the shortest month?

Answer on page 101.

UNIT 7

EXTENSION

LESSON 1

Put the words in the right order to make questions. Then answer them for you.

1 this you what going to evening are do
   Q *What are you going to do this evening?*
   A
2 you are who see going this to weekend
   Q
   A
3 going be Saturday on you night where to are
   Q
   A
4 England you visit are when to going
   Q
   A

LESSON 2

Look at the chart and write sentences about Teresa and Jake.

love ☆☆☆   not mind ☆   not like ★

	Teresa	Jake
skateboarding	★	☆☆☆
painting	☆☆☆	★
riding	☆	☆☆☆
swimming	☆☆☆	☆
dancing	☆	★
playing chess	★	☆

1 *Teresa doesn't like skateboarding, but Jake loves it.*
2
3
4
5
6

LESSON 3

Write five sentences about sports and leisure activities using the superlative form of some of these adjectives.

boring   dangerous   exciting   fast   good   popular   slow

I think that skydiving is the most exciting sport.

LESSON 4

Write a short paragraph for a visitor to your country. Talk about the best time to come, how to travel and some places to visit.

Web watch

Find out more information about countries you want to visit on the Internet. Search for 'Lonely Planet' or 'Rough Guide'.

Spelling

Correct the spelling of these words from Unit 7 by doubling one letter in each word.

1 corect (r)   2 excelent   3 girafe   4 parot   5 programe
6 rabit   7 shep   8 sugest   9 swiming   10 tenage
11 unhapy   12 woried

Brainteaser

When do two and two make more than four?

Answer on page 101.

7 Culture

Food around the world

1 Reading

Read the texts. Then match them with the photos.

1

The Costa Family, Havana, Cuba

Sandra Costa, 31, her husband Ramón, 32, and their children Lisandra, 16, and Favio, 6, live in a flat behind Ramón's father's house. Sandra is a secretary and Ramón works in a warehouse. Sandra's sister Eulina, a hairdresser, lives in the next flat. They eat meat, eggs (12 a week), fish, rice (3kg a week), potatoes (3kg a week), bread, pasta, salad, vegetables and lots of fresh fruit.

2

The Mendoza Family, Todos Santos, Guatemala

Susana Pérez Matias, 47, and Fortunato Pablo Mendoza, 50, have five children – the youngest, Marcelucía, 9, didn't want to be in the photo! Three times a day they eat rice, beans, potatoes (9kg a week), eggs (30 a week) and tortillas. Like most families in Todos Santos, they eat meat less than once a week. 'And we don't have fish because we live so far from the sea,' says Susana. Her daughter Cristolina, 19, says they don't eat sweets or cakes. 'If we want a *postre* (dessert),' she says, 'we eat a banana.' The Mendoza family eat lots of fruit and vegetables, and drink only water, not soft drinks. And they have great teeth!

3

The Batsuur Family, Ulan Bator, Mongolia

Oyuntsetseg, 38, her husband Regzen, 44, and their children Batbileg, 12, and Khorloo, 17, live in one room in a flat. Regzen is an electrician and Oyuntsetseg works in a chemist's. She buys their food in a large market in the suburbs. They share the cooking and often have meat and vegetables for dinner. The family eats a lot of eggs (30 a week) and potatoes (5kg a week). They also eat rice (2kg) and pasta (2kg).

a

b

c

Culture

2 Writing

Answer the questions.

Which …

1 husband and wife share the cooking? *Oyuntsetseg and Regzen Batsuur*
2 families eat a lot of fruit?
3 family doesn't eat a lot of meat?
4 family lives near the husband's father?
5 families eat a lot of eggs?
6 husband and wife are the oldest?
7 family has the youngest child?
8 husband works in a warehouse?
9 family eats the most potatoes?

3 Vocabulary

Label the pictures with these words.

chemist's   hairdresser   secretary   suburbs   flat   warehouse

1 _____
2 _____
3 _____
4 _____
5 _____
6 _____

4 Reading and writing

Read the texts on page 88 again. Then read the sentences and write *T* (true) or *F* (false). Correct the false sentences.

1 Sandra Costa's sister is a secretary.   *F*
   Sandra Costa's sister is a hairdresser.

2 The Mendoza family doesn't eat sweets or cakes. ☐

3 All three families eat fish. ☐

4 The Batsuur family eats lots of fresh fruit. ☐

5 Oyuntsetseg works in a warehouse. ☐

6 Lisandra is older than Khorloo. ☐

7 The Cuban family eats the most rice. ☐

8 Sandra Costa is older than her husband. ☐

9 There are four children in the Mendoza family photo. ☐

10 The Costa family eats the most eggs. ☐

8.1 HOME FROM HOME
I'd like a cold drink

1 Reading
Read the dialogue. Then complete the sentences.

ADAM Hi, Mum. I'm really hungry!
DIANA Would you like a hamburger?
ADAM No, thanks. I'd like a sandwich. Are there any sausages?
DIANA No, there aren't. But there's some cheese in the fridge and there are some tomatoes.
ADAM OK, cheese is fine.
DIANA There's some bread on the table over there. And there's some butter in the fridge.
ADAM Is there any orange juice?
DIANA Sorry – no, there isn't. There's some apple juice in the fridge and there's some milk.
ADAM No, thanks.
DIANA Would you like some ice cream?
ADAM Yes, please!

1 There aren't ___*any*___ sausages.
2 There are some _____.
3 There's _____ cheese in the fridge and there's also some _____ for the bread.
4 There isn't _____ orange juice, but there's _____ apple juice and _____ milk.
5 Adam would like _____ ice cream.

2 Countable and uncountable nouns
Complete the chart with these words.

~~apple~~   carrot   ~~food~~   hamburger   milk   orange
mushroom   pasta   porridge   potato   rice   soup

Countable nouns		Uncountable nouns
Singular	Plural	
apple	apples	food

3 some/any with countable and uncountable nouns
Look at the picture and write sentences.

1 apples — *There are some apples.*
2 oranges — *There aren't any oranges.*
3 fruit — *There's some fruit.*
4 bananas
5 glasses
6 water
7 milk
8 knife
9 spoon
10 fork
11 plate
12 cups
13 hamburgers
14 sandwiches
15 magazines
16 books
17 newspaper
18 pens

UNIT 8

4 Crossword

Look at the pictures and complete the crossword.

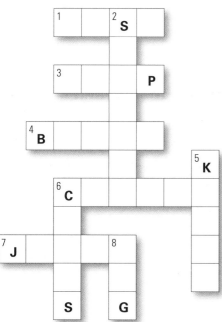

Now complete the dialogue. The numbers refer to the words in the crossword.

WAITER   What would you like to eat?
CUSTOMER   First I'd like some tomato
           (**3**) ...., please. And then
           I'd like some (**1**) .... and
           .... (**6** down).
WAITER   Do you want any (**4**) ....?
CUSTOMER   No, thank you.
WAITER   What would you like to drink?
CUSTOMER   I'd like some orange (**7**) ....,
           please.

5 Vocabulary

Match the words in list A with the words in list B to make six compound words. Then write the words.

	A	B	
1	chocolate	cream	1 *chocolate cake*
2	dish	cake	2 ....
3	fast	salad	3 ....
4	ice	food	4 ....
5	tomato	machine	5 ....
6	washing	washer	6 ....

6 Vocabulary

Complete with these words.

coffee	cooker	cup	fridge	milk
potato	thirsty	tomato	vegetarian	

1 You can make chips from a ....
2 A .... is a red fruit.
3 You drink from a ....
4 .... comes from cows.
5 When you feel ...., you want a drink.
6 A .... doesn't eat meat.
7 You cook food on a ....
8 .... is a popular hot drink.
9 You keep food cold in a ....

7 Pronunciation

Complete the chart with these words.

~~banana~~	~~barbecue~~	dishwasher	hamburger
opinion	potato	sandwiches	sausages
together	tomato	vegetable	

■ ▪ ▪	▪ ■ ▪
barbecue	*banana*

Extension Write a dialogue between a waiter and a customer in your notebook. Use the dialogue in exercise 4 to help you, but change the food and drink.

91

8.2 HOME FROM HOME
I haven't got a games console

1 Reading

Read the dialogue. Tick (✓) the things Emily and Teresa have got in their bags and cross (✗) the things they haven't got.

EMILY   This bag is really heavy!
TERESA   What have you got in there?
EMILY   Just a few things – my phone, my wallet, my sunglasses ...
TERESA   And ...?
EMILY   Well, let's see. I've also got a magazine, a bottle of water, a packet of tissues, a computer game, a banana ...
TERESA   A banana?!
EMILY   Yes, in case I get hungry.
TERESA   That's not 'just a few things'! I'm not surprised that your bag is heavy.
EMILY   OK, then, what have you got in your bag?
TERESA   Well, I haven't got a banana! Just my phone, my wallet and a packet of tissues.
EMILY   What's this, then?
TERESA   A CD. But that's all.
EMILY   No fruit?
TERESA   No!

	Emily	Teresa
banana	✓	✗
bottle of water		
CD		
computer game		
magazine		
packet of tissues		
phone		
sunglasses		
wallet		

2 *have got*: affirmative and negative

Look at the chart in exercise 1 and write sentences.

1   CD
     Teresa has got a CD. Emily hasn't got a CD.

2   wallet
     Emily and Teresa have got wallets.

3   bottle of water

4   packet of tissues

5   sunglasses

6   computer game

7   banana

8   phone

3 *have got*: affirmative and negative

Write sentences.

1   Ruby/brother ✓/sisters ✗
     Ruby has got a brother, but she hasn't got any sisters.

2   Adam and Pierre/brothers ✗

3   Diana/two children ✓

4   Teresa and Jake/brothers or sisters ✗

5   Adam/sister ✓/brothers ✗

6   Mr Ward/children ✗

UNIT 8

4 have got: questions and short answers

Write questions. Then look at the completed chart exercise 6 on page 105 of the Student's Book, and answer them.

1 Pierre/a sister
   Has Pierre got a sister?
   Yes, he has.

2 Katya/a brother

3 Adam/a skateboard

4 Katya and Teresa/pets.

5 Pierre/a pet

6 Pierre and Katya/camera phones

5 How much …?

Look at the pictures and write questions. Then answer them.

1 *How much is the laptop?*
   It's seven hundred and fifty euros.

2

3

4

5

6

6 Vocabulary

Match these words with their definitions.

> DVD player   expensive   ~~hobby~~   poster
> allowance   games console

1 Something you enjoy doing in your free time. _____hobby_____

2 You can play computer games on this. _____

3 Money that parents give their children every week or every month. _____

4 You can watch films on this. _____

5 Not cheap. _____

6 Large picture on the wall, for example, of a pop star. _____

7 Pronunciation

Complete the chart with these words.

> ~~cottage~~   ~~game~~   got   good   hamburger   magazine
> sausage   suggest   teenager   vegetarian

/g/ **girl**	/dʒ/ **orange**
game	*cottage*

Extension   In your notebook, answer the three questions in the survey on page 104 of the Student's Book for you.

1 €750
2 €150

3 €200

4 €30

5 €2

6 €8

8 HOME FROM HOME

3 It's different, isn't it?

1 Reading

Read the text. Then answer the questions.

It's a beautiful sunny day and all the students are at the barbecue at Adam and Ruby's house. They're having a great time. Steven Campbell is cooking hamburgers on the barbecue and Diana Campbell is giving plates to Pierre and Ruby. Pierre and Ruby are sitting at a table in the garden and talking. The other students are standing around talking, eating and drinking orange juice. Emily is talking to Jake. David Ward is there, too. He's talking to Diana. Katya and Adam are standing near the barbecue. They're watching Steven.

1 The students are at a barbecue, aren't they?
   Yes, they are.

2 Diana Campbell is cooking hamburgers, isn't she?
   No, she isn't. She's giving plates to Pierre and Ruby.

3 David Ward is talking to Steven, isn't he?

4 It's a rainy day, isn't it?

5 Emily is talking to Jake, isn't she?

6 Pierre and Ruby are standing up, aren't they?

2 Question tags with *be*

Look at the pictures and complete the questions.

1 She's from _____*Spain*_____, isn't she _____?

2 His name is _____, _____?

3 They're in _____, _____?

4 They're at the _____, _____?

5 She's playing the _____, _____?

6 It's a _____, _____?

3 Question tags with *be*

Complete with question tags.

1. Valencia is in Spain, *isn't it*?
2. Rafael Nadal and Roger Federer are tennis players, ...?
3. The capital of Australia is Canberra, ...?
4. Justin Bieber is a singer, ...?
5. Brighton is a nice city, ...?
6. Zac Efron and Will Smith are film stars, ...?
7. The Taj Mahal is in India, ...?
8. The mosquito is the most dangerous animal in the world, ...?
9. Fidan and Amna are at school in England, ...?
10. Luis is from Peru, ...?

4 Question tags with *be*

Match the quiz questions with the answers.

1. Which is the most dangerous animal?
2. Which is the most famous building in Brighton?
3. What is the most important food for Japanese people?
4. Who is Uma Thurman?
5. Who is Lief Eriksson?
6. Where are Devil's Dyke and the Isle of Wight?

a. It's rice, isn't it?
b. She's an actress, isn't she?
c. They're in England, aren't they?
d. It's the mosquito, isn't it?
e. He's a Viking explorer, isn't he?
f. It's the Royal Pavilion, isn't it?

5 Vocabulary

Match these words with their definitions.

sad   dad   barbecue   drop   ice cream   ~~whoops~~

1. You say this when you make a mistake. *whoops*
2. Very cold, very nice food! ....
3. Let something fall. ....
4. Masculine of *mum*. ....
5. Not happy. ....
6. A meal you cook outside. ....

6 Vocabulary

Complete with these words.

hungry   another   matter   meet   no   please   something   well

1. Nice to .... you.
2. We're getting on ....
3. Would you like .... to eat?
4. Yes, ...
5. I'm not ....
6. What's the .... ?
7. .... , thanks.
8. Would you like .... drink?

7 Pronunciation

Mark the stressed syllable.

■
beginning   confident   connected
delicious   paradise   understand

Extension What do you think Pierre and Ruby are talking about at the barbecue? Write a dialogue in your notebook using question tags.

8.4 HOME FROM HOME
Integrated Skills: Invitation and thanks

1 Reading

Read and match the invitations with the replies.

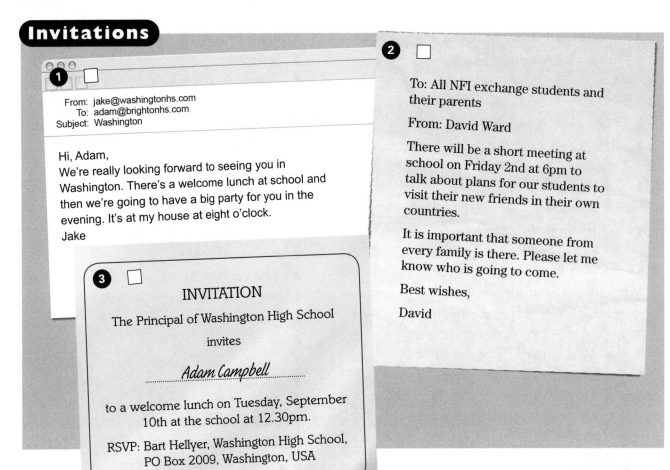

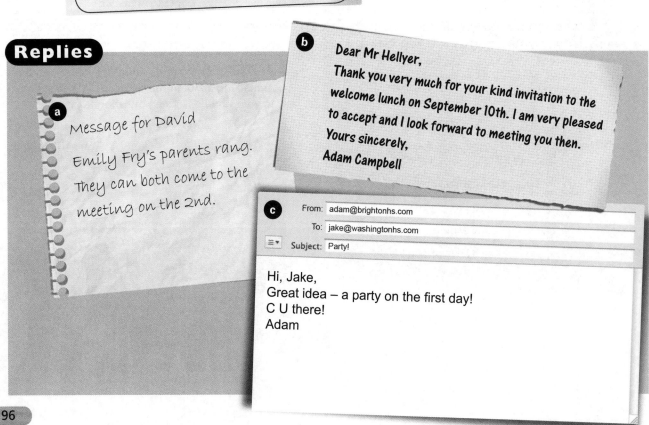

2 Writing

In your notebook, write an email to an English-speaking friend who is coming to visit your country. Invite your friend to lunch on the first day. Then write a reply from your friend.

3 Crossword

Complete the crossword.

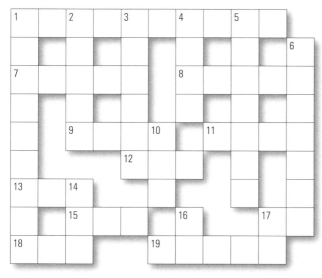

Across →

1. You can look up words in this book. (10)
7. The … of Adam's parents are Diana and Steven. (5)
8. The largest animal in the sea. (5)
9. People cross their fingers for good … (4)
11. There's a phone message from home. Please … back. (4)
12. A popular hot drink in Britain. (3)
13. Opposite of *young*. (3)
15. Is there … milk in the fridge? (3)
17. What do you like doing … your free time? (2)
18. Orlando Bloom likes …diving. (3)
19. Opposite of *best*. (5)

Down ↓

1. The mosquito is the most … animal in the world. (9)
2. You can see this animal in Egypt. (5)
3. Small animal with six legs. (6)
4. You can listen to the … on the radio. (4)
5. I love … books in my free time. (7)
6. This black and white bird can't fly. (7)
10. You can open a door with this. (3)
14. Opposite of *night*. (3)
16. What are you going … do today? (2)
17. It's a great party, isn't …? (2)

UNIT 8

LEARNER INDEPENDENCE

Learning outside the classroom

How can you practise English in the holidays? Order these suggestions from 1 (most useful) to 10 (least useful).

a Phone or text a friend in English. ☐
b Find an epal and email him/her in English. ☐
c Look back at your homework. Note the mistakes and correct them. ☐
d Make a video recording of yourself speaking English. ☐
e Read the Self Assessment sections in the Workbook again and check your progress. ☐
f Look at the Language File at the back of the Student's Book. ☐
g Look at the Word List at the back of the Student's Book and add words to your vocabulary notebook. ☐
h Talk to yourself in English when you are out for a walk. ☐
i Read the projects you did this year. ☐
j Make crossword puzzles in English for a friend to complete. ☐

Extensive reading

Read *The Black Tulip* by Alexandre Dumas. Does Cornelius create the first black tulip? Does Rosa become his wife?

1672 – The Netherlands. It's a dangerous time. People are fighting in the streets.
Cornelius loves two things. He loves tulips and he loves the beautiful Rosa.
Cornelius wants to win the prize: the prize for the first black tulip flower in the Netherlands. But Cornelius has enemies. His enemies put him in prison. He is going to die.

97

8 HOME FROM HOME

Inspiration EXTRA!

REVISION

LESSON 1

Complete with *some* or *any*.

1 Let's buy _____ fruit.
2 Are there _____ oranges?
3 Would you like _____ bread and cheese?
4 I don't want _____ potatoes.
5 There isn't _____ milk in the fridge.
6 I'd like _____ apple juice, please.
7 Is there _____ meat in the sandwiches?
8 Can I have _____ chocolate cake, please?
9 I don't want _____ pasta.
10 Let's have _____ kebabs.

LESSON 2

Complete with *have(n't) got* or *has(n't) got*.

1 I *haven't got* a pet snake. ✗
2 Emily _____ a nice room. ✓
3 Pierre _____ a brother. ✗
4 Adam _____ a camera phone. ✓
5 You _____ an epal. ✗
6 They _____ lots of DVDs. ✓
7 The word *dictionary* _____ ten letters. ✓
8 We _____ green hair. ✗
9 The Brighton High School students _____ a great gym. ✓
10 I _____ a million pounds. ✗

LESSON 3

Complete with these question tags.

isn't she   isn't he   isn't it   aren't I
aren't we   aren't you   aren't they

1 You're having fun, _____ ?
2 We're late, _____ ?
3 Teresa is Spanish, _____ ?
4 Steven is cooking, _____ ?
5 Pierre and Ruby are friends, _____ ?
6 I'm good at English, _____ ?
7 It's cold today, _____ ?

LESSON 4

Match expressions 1–5 with their meanings. Choose from a–h.

1 Hiya. [f]
2 I'm really thirsty. [ ]
3 Please let me know. [ ]
4 Wicked! [ ]
5 I'd love to. [ ]

a Can you give me your answer?
b Oh dear!
c That's terrible!
d I'd really like to do that.
e I'd like something to drink.
f Hello.
g Are you sure?
h That's great.

Spelling

Complete these words from Unit 8.

1 ac__ept 2 ap__le 3 ar__ive 4 barb__cue 5 fri__ge
6 hob__y 7 ju__ce 8 sa__sage 9 skatebo__rd
10 sug__estion 11 veget__rian 12 wi__ked

Brainteaser

Why can monkeys open doors?

Answer on page 101.

98

UNIT 8

EXTENSION

LESSON 1

Complete the dialogue about food with your own ideas.

- A What would you like to eat?
- B I'd like
- A Would you like
- B
- A Do you want
- B
- A And what would you like to drink?
- B
- A We haven't got any
    Would you like some
- B

LESSON 2

You can use both *have* and *have got* to talk about possession. Rewrite these questions using *have/has got*. Then answer them for you.

1 Do you have any pets?

   Have you got any pets?
   Yes, I've got a dog. OR   *No, I haven't.*

2 Do you have any brothers or sisters?

3 Do your parents have a car?

4 Does your school have a football team?

5 Do you have a musical instrument?

6 Does your best friend have a mobile phone?

7 Do you have red hair?

8 Does your teacher have blue eyes?

LESSON 3

Complete with question tags.

1 We're learning English, ?
2 It's quite easy, ?
3 I'm working hard, ?
4 Mr Ward is a good teacher, ?
5 Diana is Steven's wife, ?
6 The students are friendly, ?
7 You're happy, ?

LESSON 4

Yesterday you went to a party at a friend's house. Write a thank you letter to your friend's parents in your notebook.

Web watch

Go to www.bbc.co.uk/food and search for a recipe you would like to cook. Look up new words in the dictionary and add them to your vocabulary notebook.

Spelling

We add *-s* to make the plural of most nouns ending in *-o*, but three nouns below form the plural with *-es*. One of these is an insect and the other two are things you can eat.

Add *-s* or *-es* to make plural nouns.

1 disco *s*   2 euro   3 hippo   4 kilo
5 mosquito   6 photo   7 piano   8 potato
9 radio   10 tomato   11 video

Brainteaser

What two things can't you have for breakfast?

Answer on page 101.

REVIEW
Units 7–8

1 Read and complete. For each number 1–12, choose word or phrase A, B or C.

HEALTH AROUND THE WORLD

A survey by the World Health Organisation (WHO) of over 162,000 young people aged 11–15 in 35 countries tells us a lot about teenage lifestyles.

Most young people do __1__ exercise (like sport or going to the gym), but under 50% do more than five hours' exercise a week. And some teenagers don't do __2__ exercise at all. Girls don't enjoy __3__ exercise as much as boys – about 25% of girls like __4__ TV for four or more hours a day, and about 15% spend three hours a day at their computers. Young people in Canada and the USA do the most exercise.

Under 40% of teenagers eat fruit every day and only about 33% eat vegetables every day. But there are big differences between different countries. For example, the __5__ numbers of 15 year olds who eat sweets every day (40–50%) are in Belgium, Italy, Ireland and Scotland. Greece and Scandinavia __6__ the smallest number of sweet-eaters (20%).

And what do you do after eating sweets? Clean your teeth – and here there are also big differences between countries. In Switzerland, 91% of 13-year-old girls clean their teeth every day – the __7__ percentage of young people. The lowest percentage is in Malta, where 88% of 15-year-old boys hate __8__ their teeth and don't do it every day.

There are lots of differences between boys and girls in the survey. One of the __9__ differences is how they talk to their friends. In all countries, more girls than boys phone, email and text their friends.

The WHO does this survey every four years – what's __10__ change in four years' time? Are teenagers going __11__ more exercise or spend more time at their computers? It's difficult to say, __12__? What do you think?

1	**A** a	**B** some	**C** any
2	**A** a	**B** some	**C** any
3	**A** do	**B** to do	**C** doing
4	**A** watching	**B** watched	**C** watch
5	**A** large	**B** larger	**C** largest
6	**A** got	**B** has got	**C** have got
7	**A** high	**B** higher	**C** highest
8	**A** cleaning	**B** clean	**C** cleaned
9	**A** big	**B** most big	**C** biggest
10	**A** going	**B** going to	**C** go to
11	**A** to do	**B** do	**C** doing
12	**A** is it	**B** isn't it	**C** it is

2 Read the definitions and complete the words.

1. This is the tallest animal in the world. g_____
2. This sea animal has eight legs. o_____
3. This bird can speak. p_____
4. This animal lives in the Arctic. p_____
5. This bird lives in Antarctica. p_____
6. This insect is the most dangerous animal. m_____
7. This is the fastest land animal. c_____
8. This large sea animal has a long nose. d_____

100

3 Complete the dialogues. Choose A, B or C.

1 What's wrong with her?
   A She's ill.
   B No, she's right.
   C Yes, it's a mistake.

2 Do you like dancing?
   A No, I'm listening to music.
   B Yes, it's boring.
   C I don't mind it.

3 How much is it?
   A It's very big.
   B It's quite expensive.
   C There's a lot.

4 Would you like something to eat?
   A Yes, I love it.
   B No, thanks – I'm not thirsty.
   C Yes, please – I'd like a sandwich.

5 Hi, how are you?
   A I'm fine, thanks.
   B Nice to meet you.
   C My name is Adam.

4 Find the odd word.

1 adult   aunt   parent   uncle
2 ambulance   hospital   medicine   police
3 dancing   morning   painting   riding
4 camel   monkey   penguin   tiger
5 cooker   dishwasher   fridge   kitchen
6 cup   fork   knife   spoon
7 apple   banana   orange   potato
8 biggest   highest   smallest   suggest

Answers to Brainteasers

UNIT 7
Revision May.
Extension When they make 22.

UNIT 8
Revision Because they've got 'keys'.
Extension Lunch and dinner.

LEARNER INDEPENDENCE
SELF ASSESSMENT

Vocabulary

1 Draw this chart in your notebook. How many words can you write in each category?

More than 10? **Good!**   *More than 12?* **Very good!**
More than 15? **Excellent!**

Animals	
Food and drink	
Possessions	
Leisure activities	

2 Put the words in order to make expressions from the phrasebooks in Lesson 4 in Units 7 and 8.

1 with wrong him what's

2 going to what do you are

3 what you do suggest

4 know please me let

5 to party our come

6 there you see

Check your answers.
6/6 **Excellent!**   4/6 **Very good!**   2/6 **Try again!**

My learning diary
In Units 7 and 8:
My favourite topic is

My favourite picture is

The three lessons I like most are

My favourite activity or exercise is

Something I don't understand is

Something I want to learn more about is

101

L.A. ADVENTURE

4. He knows our faces!

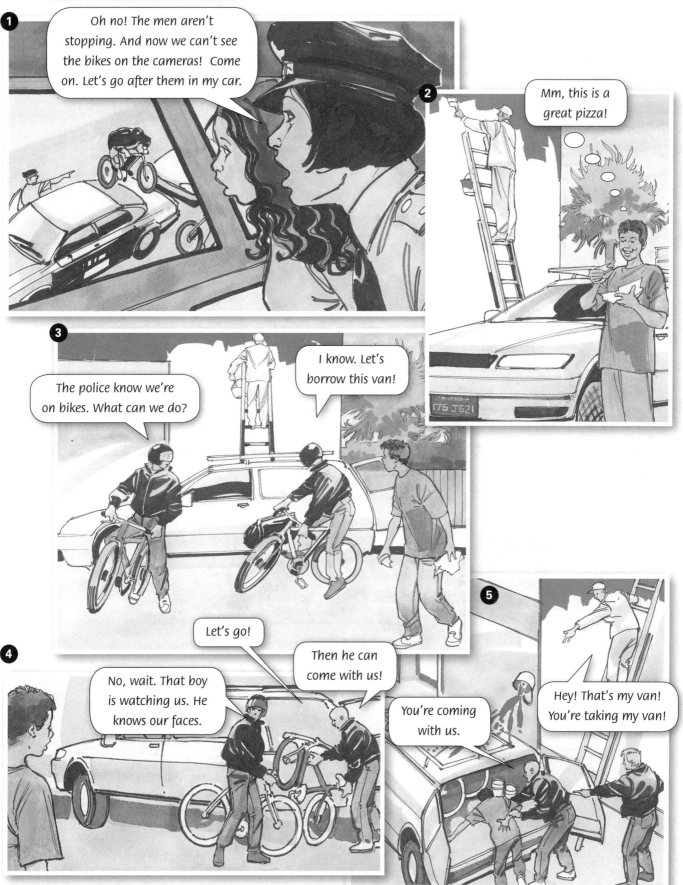

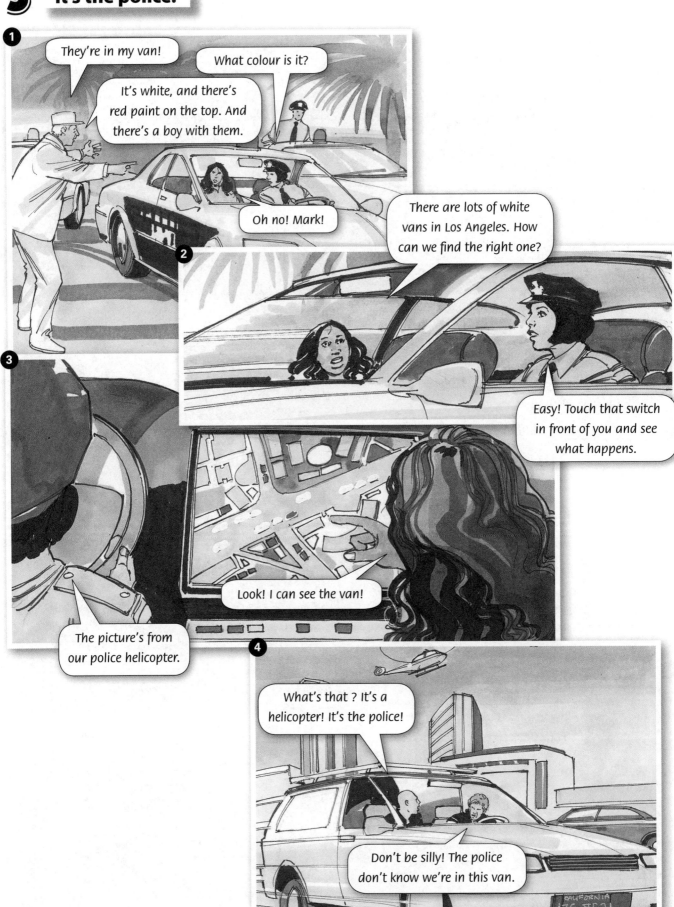

L.A. ADVENTURE

 I have an idea

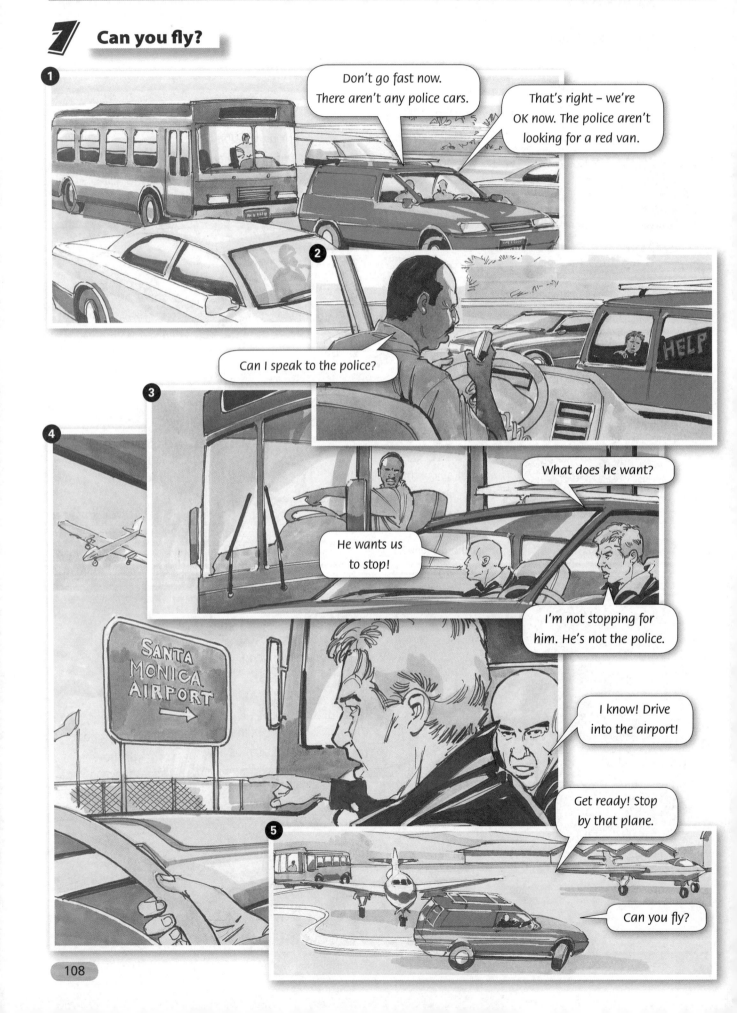

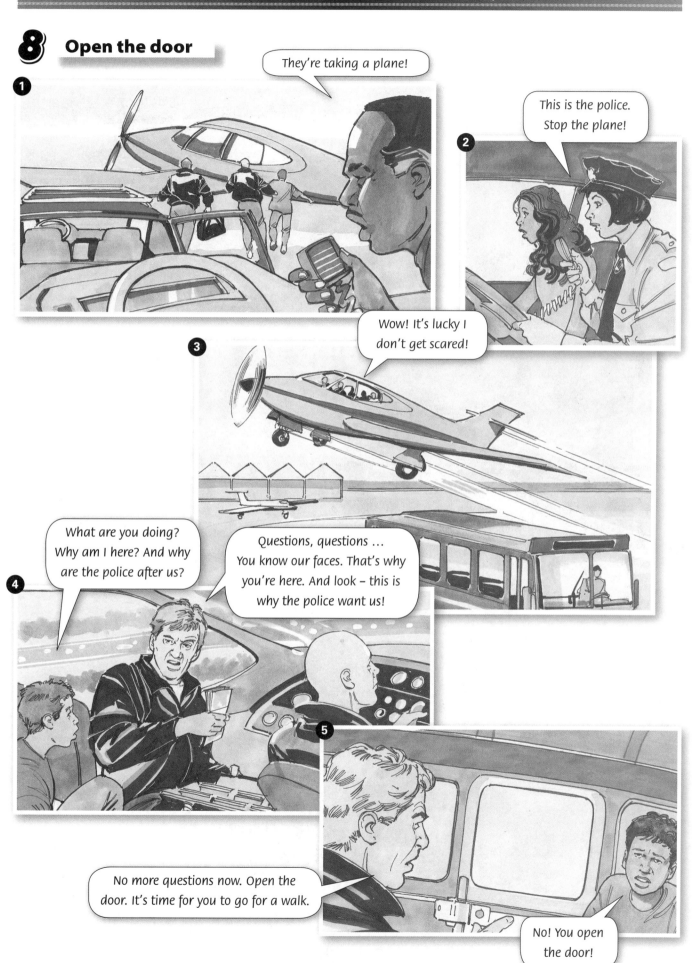

L.A. ADVENTURE EXERCISES

1 Answer the questions.

1 What's the name of Anna's brother?

2 Where are Anna and her brother from?

3 Where is their mother from?

4 Where are Anna and her brother?

2 Answer the questions with short answers.

1 Can the police officer help Anna?
   Yes, she can.

2 Can Anna find her brother?

3 Is it Anna's first time in Santa Monica?

4 Are there lots of cameras?

5 Can Anna see Mark?

3 Match the captions with pictures 2–4 on page 104.

a Anna sees her brother. ☐ 4
b The men on bikes take the money. ☐
c The police officer talks to the police cars. ☐

4 Read the sentences and write *T* (true) or *F* (false). Correct the false sentences.

1 Mark is eating a hamburger. ☐ F
   Mark is eating pizza.

2 The men borrow a police car. ☐

3 Mark sees the faces of the two men. ☐

4 The painter sees the men take his van. ☐

5 Match the captions with pictures 1–4 on page 106.

a The men see the helicopter. ☐
b The police officer and Anna talk to the painter. ☐
c Anna can see the van. ☐
d The police officer and Anna go after the van. ☐

6 Answer the questions.

1 How did the police know which van the men were in?

2 Why did the men go into the car park?

3 What did the men do to the van?

4 What did Mark write on the window?

7 Read the sentences and write *T* (true) or *F* (false). Correct the false sentences.

1 Mark and the men were in a white van. ☐

2 Mark wrote HELLO on the window. ☐

3 The bus driver spoke to the police. ☐

4 The men wanted the bus driver to stop. ☐

5 The men drove into the airport. ☐

8 Match the captions with pictures 1–5 on page 109.

a The plane flies over the bus. ☐
b Mark asks questions. ☐
c Mark says no. ☐
d The bus driver talks to the police. ☐
e The police officer talks to the men. ☐

9 Read the sentences and write *T* (true) or *F* (false). Correct the false sentences.

1 Mark opened the plane door. ☐

2 Mark hit the man with the bag. ☐

3 The pilot said Mark could have all the money. ☐

4 Mark threw the money out of the door. ☐

5 When the plane landed, Mark was happy. ☐

6 Anna said thank you to Mark. ☐

CLIL MATHS
Code breakers!

1 Vocabulary

Label the pictures with these words.

> code column pattern rectangle
> row alphabetical order zigzag

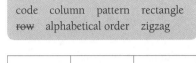
1 row

2 ....

3 ....

4 ....

5 ....

6 ....

7 ....

2 Reading

Read the text and check your answers.

What are codes?

Codes are words, numbers or signs used for sending secret messages.

How do they work?

There are a lot of ways to read and write codes, but most use just two different mathematical ideas. One is called *transposition* – this means the letters are the same as the original message, but they are in a different order or pattern. The other is called *substitution* – this is when the order or pattern is the same as the original message, but the letters are different.

Transposition codes

This is an example of a simple transposition code. To understand this type of code you need:

1 the start point (here column 1, row 1)
2 the pattern (here a zigzag)
3 the shape the code is inside (here a rectangle).

So our message here is:

B	H	B	**C**	R	A	**T**	R	L	**I**	N	C	**H**	O	F	**U**	M	P	**R**	E	N	**D**	I	N	**K**
D	**E**	S	A	**G**	E	P	**U**	C	O	**S**	T	L	**E**	R	O	**M**	A	F	**I**	O	P	**U**	N	Y
Q	U	**C**	K	V	**W**	F	E	**E**	X	F	**J**	I	P	**W**	Z	U	**A**	N	Y	**S**	T	I	L	**B**

Be careful of the woman in pink!

Difficult transposition codes use a secret word, e.g. *friend*. You number the letters in the secret word according to their order in the alphabet. For the word *friend*, the numbers are: 3 6 4 2 5 1 (*d* comes first in the alphabet so it's number 1, *e* comes second, *f* comes third, etc.). You then use these numbers as the key for reading the code. Here is the coded message:

> ETANE AOOPC BFHNK CLWNB RFMID EUEIA

To understand this code, you write the secret word in a table (one letter in each column). In the next row, you write the numbers. Now you write the letters from the secret message in the correct column.

There are six 'words' in the coded message and letter 1 in the first word is *E*, so you write this under number 1 in the table. Letter 1 in the second word is *A*, so you write this under number 2, and so on. When the row is complete, you start again on the next row. So letter 2 of the first word is *T*, letter 2 of the second word is *O*, etc. The final letters are in alphabetical order so it is clear where the message ends.

F	R	I	E	N	D
3	6	4	2	5	1
B	E	C	A	R	E
F	U	L	O	F	T
H	E	W	O	M	A
N	I	N	P	I	N
K	A	B	C	D	E

Be careful of the woman in pink!

Substitution codes

To understand substitution codes, think of letters A–Z as numbers 0–25.

A	B	C	D	E	F	G	H	I	J	K	L	M
0	1	2	3	4	5	6	7	8	9	10	11	12
N	O	P	Q	R	S	T	U	V	W	X	Y	Z
13	14	15	16	17	18	19	20	21	22	23	24	25

A simple way to make a code is to move each letter of the alphabet three places. For example, the letter *B* is number 1, and 1 + 3 = 4. The number 4 is the letter *E*. So in the code, the letter *B* changes to the letter *E*. So our message 'Be careful of the woman in pink' becomes:

EH FDUHIXO RI WKH ZRPDQ LQ SLQN

Different types of substitutions are possible. For example, moving each letter forward five places (*A* becomes *F*, *B* becomes *G*, etc.), or moving each letter back two places (*A* becomes *Y*, *B* becomes *Z*, etc.).

Cracking the codes

This information can help us to 'crack' or read a message in code:
- There are only two English words with one letter: *I* and *a*.
- *The* and *and* are very common three letter words.
- Many questions start with one of the *Wh-*question words (*What, Where, When, Who*).
- The letters *e* and *t* are very common letters in English.
- The letters *z* and *q* are not very common.

3 Reading and writing

Can you crack these codes? Complete the information about how the code works and write an answer using the same code in your notebook.

1

L	U	N	C
S	D	Y	H
I	K	A	?
N	E	**H**	**W**

Message: *Wh*
Type of code: (**transposition**) / substitution
Start: *column 4, row 4*
Pattern: *circle*   Shape: *square*

2

W	J	E	G	I	R	O	P	U	T	S	D	M	I	N
C	**H**	E	T	Y	S	B	O	G	R	E	A	P	E	S
K	R	A	E	T	U	Y	L	I	F	N	G	C	H	?

Message: *Wh*
Type of code: **transposition / substitution**
Start: _____
Pattern: _____   Shape: _____

3

FQJC RB HXDA OJEXDARCN LXUXDA?

Message: *Wh*
Type of code: **transposition / substitution**
Pattern: *+9*

4

DKS KHZ EO PDA LANOKJ JATP PK UKQ?

Message: *How*
Type of code: **transposition / substitution**
Pattern: _____

5

TRA SAD IEC HYB IVS SEY

Message: _____
Type of code: **transposition / substitution**
Key word: orange
Numbers: ___ , ___ , *1* , ___ , *3* , *2*

O	R	A	N	G	E
		1			

4 Project

Write some codes for your classmates to crack.
- Write some easy and some difficult codes.
- Write some transposition and some substitution codes.
- Use codes with key words.
- Try inventing a new code.

CLIL DRAMA
AFTER 4 Theatre design

1 Reading

Read the text and match these words with the pictures.

a proscenium/traditional stage
b end stage
c arena stage
d open stage

1 [c]

2 Reading and writing

Read the text again and complete the chart.

Type of stage	Good things 😊	Bad things ☹
arena stage	audience is close to actors	no scenery changes or special effects
open stage		
end stage		
proscenium/traditional stage		

A theatre designer's job is to decide how a play looks to an audience. The 'look' of a play depends on many things: the type of stage (the place where the actors stand), the scenery (what we can see behind the actors), the lighting (the colour and position of the lights), the costumes (what the actors wear) and the special effects (the images or sounds which make the play exciting). All these things help the audience to understand and enjoy the play.

There are four types of stage. An *arena* stage is one where the audience is sitting or standing on all four sides. The audience is very close to the actors, but you can't change the scenery or have lots of special effects because the audience can always see every part of the stage.

An *open* stage is when the audience is sitting on three sides of the stage. The audience is always close to the actors, but scenery changes and special effects are easy because there is a backstage area that the audience can never see. They can see the other people in the audience though!

When there is an *end* stage, the audience is only on one side of the stage. There can be many difficult scenery changes and special effects. The audience can only see the stage in front of them – and not the other people in the audience, so they only think about the play. However, they are usually a long way from the actors.

A *proscenium*, or *traditional*, stage has an arch between the audience and the stage. The actors often act at the front of the stage so there is space at the back of the stage for changing scenes and making special effects. But many people in the audience are a long way from the actors.

Lighting is another very important part of theatre design because it can show the time of day, the place and the feeling of that place. For example, we use dark colours to show it is nighttime and bright colours to show it is daytime. We can tell the audience what to look at by only putting a light on one character or one part of the stage. Lighting is an important part of many special effects. Together with sound effects, lighting can help to create fire, fog or even a big explosion!

Scenery and costumes show the audience when and where the action is happening. For example, if a scene takes place in Roman times, the scenery and costumes look like this:

114

2 ☐   3 ☐   4 ☐

3 Vocabulary

Label the picture with these words.

actor audience backstage ~~scenery~~
special effect lighting stage costume

4 Project

Be a theatre designer for your own play! First, think about these things:

- the title of your play
- the time and place of your play (e.g. night/day, in Roman times, a stormy night, in an old house, etc.)
- the story of your play (who are the main characters and what happens to them?)

Now draw pictures to show the look of your play. Draw these things:

- the type of stage (where is the audience?)
- the scenery (also think about lighting and special effects)
- the costumes

CLIL HISTORY

6 The Incas

AFTER

1 Reading

Read the sentences and guess *T* (true) or *F* (false). Then read the text on page 117 and check your answers.

1 The Incas were from North America.   *F*
2 They lived from the 12th to the 16th centuries.   ☐
3 Another name for the Incas is the 'children of the sun'.   ☐
4 They lived in the Himalayan Mountains.   ☐
5 They wore clothes made of alpaca wool.   ☐
6 They killed animals and humans to say thank you to their gods.   ☐
7 They loved silver.   ☐

2 Vocabulary

Read the text again and match the words with the pictures.

a alpaca   b gold   c panpipes   d temple

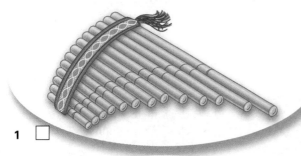

1 ☐

2 ☐

3 ☐

4 ☐

3 Reading and writing

Complete the chart with information about the Incas' lives.

1	Where in the world did they live?	They lived in the Andes mountains in South America – where Bolivia, Chile, Ecuador, Peru and parts of Argentina and Columbia are today.
2	What did they eat?	
3	What was their religion like?	
4	What clothes did they wear?	
5	What work did they do?	

HOW THE INCAS LIVED

The Incas lived in the Andes Mountains in South America – where Bolivia, Chile, Ecuador, Peru and parts of Argentina and Colombia are today. It was called 'the land of the four quarters' because the Incas ruled it in four parts: north, south, west and east. They built their capital in the middle and called it Cuzco, which means 'centre'.

From the 12th century until the Spanish arrived in the 16th century, there were about 12 million Inca people. The Incas believed they were sons of *Inti*, god of the sun, so they were also called the 'children of the sun'. The Inca leader was very important and the workers helped him by working in his army or on his land, or by building roads for him. There were a lot of rules for Inca people, but the leader looked after them when they needed food, medicine, homes or clothes.

Their homes were simple stone buildings, but the Incas also built beautiful palaces, temples and squares like those we can see today at Machu Picchu in Peru. Most people grew vegetables, corn and chillies to eat, and used the wool of animals like alpacas and llamas to make clothes. You could see how important or rich a person was by their clothes.

The Incas believed in gods of nature and had *huacas* – special places or objects like temples or statues. During religious festivals, they killed animals and even humans to give thanks to the gods. They loved gold because they thought it was a present from the god of the sun. They also loved music and played an instrument made of wood called the panpipes.

4 Project

Research another group of people from the past, for example: the Aztecs, the Celts, the Egyptians or the Romans. Use the questions in exercise 3 to help you. You can also research other things, like leisure activities, transport or education.

You can visit these websites to help you:
http://www.bbc.co.uk/history/forkids
http://www.historyforkids.org
http://www.britishmuseum.org/explore/young_explorers/discover.aspx
http://www.aztecs.org.uk/en/index.html
http://aztecs.mrdonn.org

AFTER 8 CLIL SCIENCE
Mosquitoes and malaria

1 Vocabulary

Label the pictures with these words.

blood   itchy   saliva   ~~medicine~~   mosquito net   skin   sweat

1 *medicine*   2 _____   3 _____   4 _____

 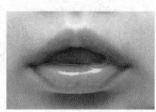

5 _____   6 _____   7 _____

2 Reading

Read the sentences and guess *T* (true) or *F* (false). Then read the text and check your answers.

1 Mosquitoes in Europe and North America usually carry malaria. ☐
2 About one million people die of malaria every year. ☐
3 It isn't possible to cure or stop malaria. ☐
4 A mosquito's mouth is like an elephant's trunk. ☐
5 Only female mosquitoes drink blood. ☐
6 Mosquitoes can smell people. ☐
7 Mosquitoes don't just carry malaria; they have malaria, too. ☐

For people living in hot tropical areas such as sub-Saharan Africa, South and South-east Asia, and Central and South America, mosquitoes are the most dangerous animals. This is because the diseases they carry, like malaria, can kill people.

Malaria is one of the world's biggest killers, with about one million deaths and 250 million people infected every year. Many of these people are young African children. It is possible to cure and stop malaria with cheap and simple medicines and mosquito nets, but many poor people don't have these things. There are also chemicals which kill mosquitoes, but mosquitoes are food for animals like frogs, bats, birds and fish, so killing them all is not the best solution.

The mosquito is like a small fly with two wings, a thin body, six long legs and a mouth like an elephant's trunk. Male and female mosquitoes use this long mouth to feed on nectar, a liquid that comes from flowers and plants. Only the female mosquito's mouth can break through an animal's or a human's skin and feed on its blood. There are some special things in the blood that she needs to make eggs.

Mosquitoes find people to feed on by looking for body heat, movement, sweat and carbon dioxide (CO_2), which animals breathe out. When a mosquito drinks blood, the person can't usually feel her do it. But the mosquito puts her saliva into the person's body and this makes the skin go red and itchy.

Mosquitoes carry diseases from one person to another, but they don't have the disease themselves. So the female mosquito drinks blood from a person with malaria and carries the disease in her body. She then bites another person without malaria, the disease enters the person's body and they get the disease too. This cycle happens many times and that is why millions of people get malaria each year.

3 Reading and writing

Read the text again and complete the information.

a   Complete the malaria facts and label the areas on the map where there is malaria.

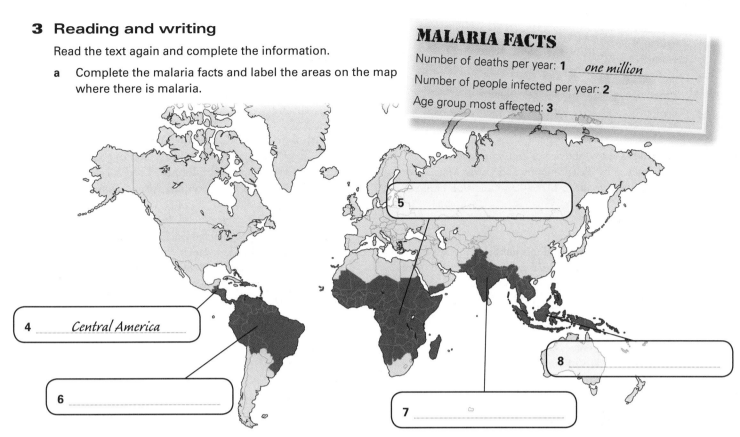

MALARIA FACTS

Number of deaths per year: **1** _one million_
Number of people infected per year: **2** _____
Age group most affected: **3** _____

4 _Central America_
5 _____
6 _____
7 _____
8 _____

b   Label the mosquito's body parts and complete the mosquito facts.

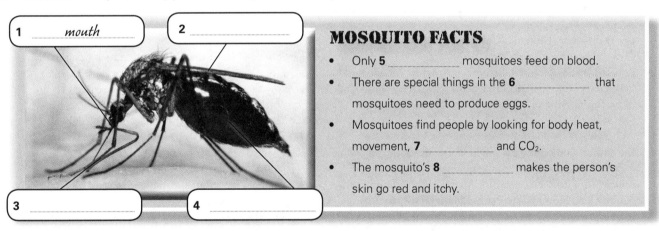

1 _mouth_   **2** _____   **3** _____   **4** _____

MOSQUITO FACTS

- Only **5** _____ mosquitoes feed on blood.
- There are special things in the **6** _____ that mosquitoes need to produce eggs.
- Mosquitoes find people by looking for body heat, movement, **7** _____ and CO_2.
- The mosquito's **8** _____ makes the person's skin go red and itchy.

c   Use these sentences to complete the malaria cycle.

a   She carries the malaria in her body.
b   Malaria enter the person's body.
c   She bites another person without malaria.

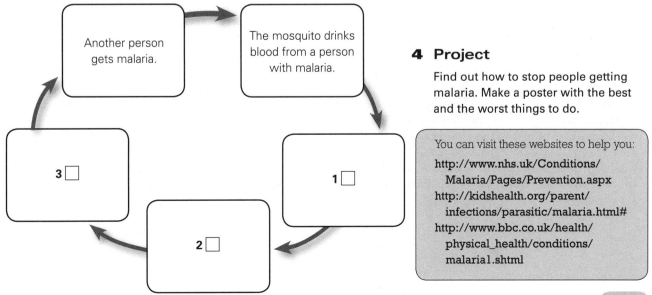

4 Project

Find out how to stop people getting malaria. Make a poster with the best and the worst things to do.

You can visit these websites to help you:

http://www.nhs.uk/Conditions/Malaria/Pages/Prevention.aspx
http://kidshealth.org/parent/infections/parasitic/malaria.html#
http://www.bbc.co.uk/health/physical_health/conditions/malaria1.shtml

Macmillan Education Limited
4 Crinan Street
London N1 9XW

Companies and representatives throughout the world

ISBN 978-0-230-41254-5

Text © Judy Garton-Sprenger, Philip Prowse 2011
Additional text by Helena Gomm and Catrin Morris 2011
Design and illustration © Macmillan Education Limited 2011

First published 2011

All rights reserved; no part of this publication may be reproduced, stored in a retrieval system, transmitted in any form, or by any means, electronic, mechanical, photocopying, recording, or otherwise, without the prior written permission of the publishers.

Original design by Giles Davies
Page make-up by D&J Hunter
Illustrated by Adrian Barclay (pp 7, 13, 19, 49, 81); Kathy Baxendale (pp 66, 116, 119); Mark Brierley (pp 22, 35, 51, 60, 98); Colin Brown (p 63); Mark Davis (pp 64, 65); Clive Goodyer (pp 21, 55); Bob Harvey (pp 102-110); Tim Kahane (pp 42, 44); Gillian Martin (pp 6, 14, 18, 23, 30, 33, 43*r*, 45, 56, 59, 70, 79, 89, 93); Peter Richardson (p 72); Gary Wing (pp 39, 43*l*, 68, 76, 90, 91, 115).
Cover design by Designers Collective
Cover photos by **Alamy**/ Mark Beton/ England (tl), Alamy/ Robert Harding Picture Library (bcl), **Corbis**/ Moodboard (tcl), **Getty**/ (bl), Getty/ Oliver Benn (tcr), Getty/ Peter Cade (bcr), **Jupiter**/ Brand X Pictures (br), **Photolibrary**/ Eric Sanford (tr).

The authors and publishers would like to thank the following for permission to reproduce their photographic material:
Alamy/Tom Brakefield p94(br), Alamy/Judith Collins p7(tl), Alamy/Chris Howes/Wild Places Photography p50, Alamy/ Corbis Premium RF p82(2), Alamy/Reinhard Dirscherl p82(8), Alamy/fStop p118(bl), Alamy/D. Hurst p7(c), Alamy/ Idealink Photography p84(b), Alamy/Tim Jones p70, Alamy/ MBI p40(tl), Alamy/nagelestock.com p15(l), Alamy/David O'Shea p115(tl), Alamy/Anne-Marie Palmer p118(tr), Alamy/ PCL p16(tl), Alamy/Photoshot Holdings Ltd p119, Alamy/ Wolfgang Pölzer p82(3), Alamy/Dave Porter p12(tr), Alamy/ Radius Images p118(cb), Alamy/Paul Rapson p16(br), Alamy/ Robert Harding Picture Library Ltd p12(br), Alamy/Chris Rout p118(tcr), Alamy/Clive Sawyer p17, Alamy/Stephen Saks Photography p16(cl), Alamy/S C Photos p8, Alamy/Nicholas Stubbs p118(br); **BBC Motion Gallery** p94(tr); **Cody Images** p84(ct); **ComStock** p118(tl); **Corbis**/Utpal Baruah/Reuters p83, Corbis/David Cheshire/Loop Images p40(tr), Corbis/ Robert Eric p115(c), Corbis/Tom Grill p100, Corbis/John Guistina p82(4), Corbis/Ian Hay at London Aerial Photo/ London Aerial Photo Library p16(bl), Corbis/Image Source p90, Corbis/Douglas Kirkland p11, Corbis/Massimo Listri p118(tcl), Corbis/Francis G. Mayer p48(b), Corbis/Kelly Redinger/Design Pics p41, Corbis/Max Rossi/Reuters p3(bl), Corbis/Denis Scott p82(6), Corbis/Marion Stalens p114(b); **Digital Stock**/Corbis p15(r); **Digital Vision** pp67, 82(1); **Getty** pp3(cr), 24, 112-113, 117, Getty/Geoff du Feu p82(7), Getty/ Fuse p7(ccl), Getty/Eri Morita p40(br), Getty/Lucy Rawlinson p48(t), Getty/Rubberball p34(l), Getty/Thinkstock Images p10, Getty/WireImage p3(br); **Image Source** p84(c); **Lonely Planet** p87(l); **Macmillan Education Ltd**/Paul Bricknell p7(ccr), Macmillan Education Ltd/Stuart Cox pp 2, 4, 5, 6, 10(b), 12(portraits), 20, 28, 34(r), 38, 54, 58, 63, 78, 92, 94(tl,ml,bl,mr), 95, Macmillan Education Ltd/David Tolley/ Dean Ryan p13(l), Macmillan Education Ltd/Dean Ryan p7(tr); **Peter Menzel**/www.menzelphoto.com p88; **Merlin Entertainments** pp46, 51; **Photolibrary** p40(bl), Photolibrary/ age fotostock p52, Photolibrary/Bridge p75, Photolibrary/ Fresh Food Images p99, Photolibrary/Imagebroker.net p82(5), Photolibrary/Imagebroker RF p16(tr), Photolibrary/ Oxford Scientific p84(t), Photolibrary/Photononstop p84(cb), Photolibrary/View Pictures p114(t); **Rex Features** pp3(tl), 39(r), Rex Features/Matt Baron/BEI pp27, 80(br), Rex Features/Alex J. Berliner/BEI p80(tr), Rex Features/Jonathan Hordle p80(l), Rex Features/Kimmo Mantyla p115(r), Rex Features/Heathcliff O'Malley p37(t), Rex Features/Sipa Press p36, Rex Features/ Startraks Photo p3(tr), Rex Features/Ray Tang p39(l); **Rough Guides Ltd** p87(r); **The Guide Dogs for the Blind Association**/ www.guidedogs.org.uk p32.

Macmillan Readers covers
Blue Fins, cover image: Alamy/ Patrick Eden p13(r)
L.A. Detective, cover image: Mark Oldroyd p25
Shooting Stars, cover image: Photodisc p37(b)
The Lost Ship, cover image: Alamy p49
The Truth Machine, cover image: Alamy, p61
The House in the Picture and Abbot Thomas' Treasure, cover image: Digital Vision p73
Dracula, cover image: Corbis p74
Jane Eyre, cover image: Auguste Macke, Bridgeman Art Library/ Getty p85
The Black Tulip, cover image: Alamy p97

The author and publishers are grateful for permission to reprint the following copyright material:
Extracts/photos of Costa, Batsuur and Mendoza families by Peter Menzel, copyright (s) Peter Menzel/ www.petermenzelphoto.com from publication entitled 'Hungry Planet: What the World Eats', reprinted with permission.

These materials may contain links for third party websites. We have no control over, and are not responsible for, the contents of such third party websites. Please use care when accessing them.

Although we have tried to trace and contact copyright holders before publication, in some cases this has not been possible. If contacted we will be pleased to rectify any errors or omissions at the earliest opportunity.

Printed and bound in Poland by CGS

2025 2024 2023 2022
33 32 31 30 29 28 27